Betrayal in Psychotherapy and Its Antidotes: Challenges for Patient and Therapist

Betrayal in Psychotherapy and Its Antidotes: Challenges for Patient and Therapist

E. Mark Stern
Editor
Iona College, New Rochelle, New York

The Haworth Press, Inc.
New York • London • Norwood (Australia)

Betrayal in Psychotherapy and Its Antidotes: Challenges for Patient and Therapist has also been published as *The Psychotherapy Patient*, Volume 8, Numbers 3/4 1992.

The Haworth Press, Inc., 10 Alice Street, Binghamton, NY 13904-1580, USA

Library of Congress Cataloging-in-Publication Data

Betrayal in psychotherapy and its antidotes : challenges for patient and therapist / E. Mark Stern, editor.
     p. cm.
     "Also . . . published as The Psychotherapy patient, volume 8, numbers 3/4, 1992"-T.p. verso.
     Includes bibliographical references.
     ISBN 1-56024-448-8 (H : acid free paper)
     1. Betrayal–Psychological aspects. 2. Psychotherapist and patient. 3. Psychotherapy. I. Stern, E. Mark, 1929- .
RC489.B45B48 1992
616.89'14–dc20   92-45159
                                                                        CIP

Betrayal in Psychotherapy and Its Antidotes: Challenges for Patient and Therapist

Betrayal in Psychotherapy and Its Antidotes: Challenges for Patient and Therapist

CONTENTS

ABOUT THE EDITOR

E. Mark Stern, EdD, is Professor in the Graduate School of Arts and Sciences, Iona College, New Rochelle, New York. A Diplomate in Clinical Psychology of the American Board of Professional Psychology and a Fellow of the American Psychological Association and the American Psychological Society, Dr. Stern is Past President of the Division of Humanistic Psychology, APA. He is in private practice of psychotherapy with offices in New York City and Dutchess County, New York. Dr. Stern completed his clinical studies at Columbia University (1955) and at the Institute of the National Psychological Association for Psychoanalysis.

Betrayal in Psychotherapy and Its Antidotes: Challenges for Patient and Therapist

Betrayal as Focus
(A Preface)

Sometimes perspectives seem like a myriad of disparate-separate dots–blotches within our landscapes. We continually strive with love, faith, trust, and determination to see–to experience–to become–the integrated whole. Life never ceases in the terrifying, enriching, compelling, creative challenges it presents. The important unifying thread is our unfailing willingness to persevere.

Virginia Fraser Stern

The larger focus is easily lost, considering that the road to hell is most often paved with shortsighted sincerity. The betrayal of humanity most commonly appears to mean less to most people than the abandonment of their long-held biases. Most members of the Nazi party claimed to simply be doing their part. The Nazis were, by common definition, a faithful lot.

The practice of psychotherapy supports and advises its clientele on a vast variety of partisan issues. Is it any wonder then that many psychotherapy patients, though feeling betrayed, rarely claim the role of betrayer? Given the benefit of the doubt, most betrayals are born free of any conscious duplicity or deceit. All the more reason that the psychotherapist should find it fitting and right to promote essential principles of common decency. As an honest broker, the therapist's methodology is obligated to help allow the most victimized to appreciate the serendipitous aspects of the betrayal process. This task is most often obscured in the so-called morally neutral sanctum of couch and consultation, although less so in couple, family and group settings.

The betrayed patient, if asked might well regard life as being

xiii

short on fairness. And so it is! But as hesitant as it might be on making sure that each one is given the appropriate due, a much less obvious truth also lives. Life is ultimately just. But this justice requires a discrete courage and patience, an ability to see more than the usual vista. The betrayed have this as their task: to focus on their respective regenerative potentialities; to each day make some attempt to appreciate the ever enlarging biosphere which includes them quite as much as did the often life-denying system of their formative years; and finally, to glare into the most evil of the injustices and betrayals, and through them, into the vastness, variety and wisdom which insight and a growing faith in life can all the more provide.

E. Mark Stern
Editor

What Is Betrayal in Psychotherapy?

James F. T. Bugental
G. Kenneth Bradford

SUMMARY. In asking what betrayal is in psychotherapy, this article inquires into the most essential meaning betrayal has for patients and therapists committed to the process of depth psychotherapy. A range of possible betrayals are discussed and the subjective import of betrayal is distinguished from the more objective arguments and judgments construing betrayals narrowly as incidents of unethical behavior on the part of therapists. Through the presentation of several case examples, the point is established that the most profound betrayal or fidelity in psychotherapy is related to the therapist striving to remain true to the genuine potentiality of a client, which can involve the therapist remaining true to what is evoked in him or her during the work.

Several recent publications have chronicled the unethical actions of mental health and other human service professionals. While many of these reports concern psychotherapists' specifically sexual involvements with clients (Pope, 1988, 1990; Rutter, 1989), it is manifest that there are other dimensions in which clients' trust may be betrayed as well. In this paper, we will explore the issue of

James F. T. Bugental, PhD, is internationally recognized as a leading exponent of Existential-Humanistic psychology and psychotherapy. He is a Diplomate in Clinical Psychology, ABPP, and is the author of numerous publications in the field, including a recent book, *Intimate Journeys*. Mailing address: 24 Elegant Tern Rd., Novato, CA 94949.

G. Kenneth Bradford earned a PhD in psychology from Saybrook Institute. He is in private practice as an Existential-Analytic psychotherapist and on the Core Faculty at John F. Kennedy University in the Graduate School for the Study of Human Consciousness. Mailing address: 70 Flora Court, Pleasant Hill, CA 94523.

1

psychotherapist betrayal in general terms and endeavor to bring out underlying principles that may be useful to therapists and to our larger professional community.

We consider betrayal to be, first and most basically, a failure in the interpersonal, or inter-*subjective,* relation between therapist and client. This is in contrast to the attitude which considers betrayal as an ethical or legal infraction which may be identified in the objective actions or non-actions of the professional, and perhaps even adjudicated through "objective" jurists.

If we are to examine a therapeutic engagement to assess whether there has been some measure of betrayal, we must establish a model against which to make this judgment. According to the priorities of depth psychotherapies in general, we propose that *an optimum client-therapist relation is one that remains true to the client's attempt to realize his or her potential as a human being.* This squarely puts the responsibility on the therapist, since the client is not always in a position to make this judgment.

Further, clarifying the optimum conditions for psychotherapy which is oriented toward the client's realization of his or her potential or for fundamental life change goes beyond the objective identification of a particular incident or action, to call for consideration of what may be most productive or healthful for the client in the long run. This is not the same as whether the therapy is "successful," but it is a more realistic parallel to that goal.

What then becomes most crucial for a positive therapeutic outcome is for the therapist to elicit and contain the emergence of a client's subjective potentiality. When this approach to therapy is paramount, then what is most at stake in the work has less to do with a preconceived final outcome than it does with the therapy being true to the process of cultivating subjective presence and responsivity. It is from this perspective that we can speak of a therapeutic *praxis* which is to some degree true to this project or which to some degree betrays it.

Prior to addressing the subtleties of therapeutic betrayal, it is incumbent upon us to situate this discussion within a clinical context by outlining a nominal range of possible clinical betrayals. In addition to *sexual misconduct* charges, the other most commonly reported ethical violations are instances of *financial exploitation.*

These actions may involve billing for services not rendered or charging excessively for emergency contacts or late payments. This could also involve the waiving or excessive reduction of fees for clients whom the therapist is in some way dependent upon. For example, the therapist may have a "rescue fantasy" in regard to a particular client, and in the process of realizing this fantasy by waiving the fee, may strip the client of that possibility for autonomous initiative.

Fraudulent advertising or professional misrepresentation are usually deliberate forms of misleading a client into placing a false confidence in a therapist. If discovered, such fraudulence is usually experienced as betrayal. Or again, there are betrayals of confidentiality, in which a therapist divulges information about a client to others who know or are in a position to know that person. The damage done to career politicians, for example, whose past psychological treatment is made public, is obviously far-reaching. Less visibly, it is also not uncommon for patients seen in institutional settings to become aware of the clinical gossip on a ward or in a center, and to feel dehumanized by such "shop talk."

Under the general rubric of "countertransference," a variety of forms of therapeutic *process betrayal* can occur as a therapist neglects a client's therapeutic project. This may occur by continually being distracted during a session, perhaps by thinking about one's own concerns on a client's time, or more grossly by using the client to ventilate one's own problems (the clinical equivalent to "parentification"). For example, even though a primary focus of the therapy was devoted to Vicki's tendency to care for others at great emotional expense to herself, her therapist still used her as his personal confidante, and intimated that he cared deeply for her. When Vicki told the therapist of her budding love for him and of her confusion regarding the overfriendly nature of their "professional" client-therapist relationship, this therapist coolly withdrew and minimized her perception. Vicki, feeling betrayed, quit therapy soon thereafter. A therapist herself, Vicki recognized a double betrayal. She felt both exploited by having the therapist use her to assuage his own loneliness and then abandoned when he emotionally withdrew from her following the confrontation.

In this regard, we can also speak of *relational betrayal,* or a sabotage of the therapeutic "container." Instances in which a therapist adopts a dual relationship with a client which compromises the therapist's neutrality and confounds his or her specifically therapeutic responsibility toward the client can be cited. Also, instances in which the therapist knows something of his or her own life circumstances which may threaten the course of therapy and withholds that information can be forms of therapeutic betrayal. For example, when one plans to leave a geographical area or discovers that one has a terminal illness and fails to inform one's clients of such impending events, one violates the implicit trust that a course of therapy will be able to uninterruptedly run its course.

Even without making an exhaustive list, it is apparent that violations of trust can occur in many different ways within a therapeutic relationship. More difficult is rating the relative gravity of each form of betrayal. While the recent literature would seem to imply that sexual misconduct is the most severe, we contend that the gravity of the violation is less dependent on the objective act than it is on the subjective impact of a betrayal. In this we are in accord with Freudian psychoanalysis, which suggests it is not the disturbing *event* per se that is traumatic, but that it is the *experience* of the event, how one takes it (in) that is traumatic.

A case example: Sarah entered psychoanalysis with a well-respected analyst, Dr. R., with an explicit agreement that the therapy would be permitted to follow its natural course through to a (hopefully) successful conclusion. Unbeknownst to Sarah, the therapist fell ill to a fatal disease during the course of the therapy and later died suddenly without warning. Sarah felt deeply betrayed by this turn of events, since it violated her expectation of her therapeutic project and even recapitulated a traumatic childhood abandonment. Immediately prior to his sudden resignation from clinical practice and subsequent death, Sarah confronted Dr. R. regarding his being tardy for their sessions. His response to this was to fly into a rage and strongly reprimand her. Upon finding out that she was not only precluded from working out this dispute with him, but that he had known for some time that he had a fatal disease that would eventually abort therapy with all of his analysands and did not disclose this ominous fact, Sarah fell into a severe abandonment depression.

Greg, another patient of the same therapist, also felt deeply betrayed by Dr. R. for denying him the chance to work through issues related to terminating therapy. However, in Greg's case, the felt severity of the betrayal did not cripple his positive responsivity to the event. He was able to join an informal group of other analysands who were in the same situation and to use this tragic event to confront on a deeper level his persistent dependency issues. Both Sarah and Greg felt betrayed and abandoned, but the meaning, gravity, and proximal outcome of the betrayal was quite different for each. Even though the objective event was the same for both, the subjective experience was different. This is the difference which makes all the difference.

The objective event of an incident such as betrayal is always subordinate to the primacy of the lived, subjective experience. What is most at stake, and likely to be betrayed, during depth therapy is nothing as objectively specifiable as a clinical treatment plan or a preconceived design to become a better person, but the therapeutic possibility of being present to one's actual, embodied experience.

The primary assumption to which we adhere affirms that fundamental therapeutic transformation occurs from within (Bradford, 1989; Bugental, 1968, 1978, 1990). While this may sound a bit trite or obvious, in practice it is still one of the most difficult therapeutic axioms to remain true to. "I" can change only when "I" am on the line, engaged in the wrenching, often confusing, terrifying, and wondrous process of being present to that latent potentiality which eludes me. What is thus most necessary in the practice of intensive psychotherapy is to aid a client in contacting, recognizing, and realizing his or her subjective potentiality, even if this potency presents itself initially as a disturbance, symptom, or resistance.

The therapist's challenge becomes one of maintaining fidelity to the client's subjective process, since there is the implicit, and sometimes explicit, agreement on the part of the therapist to remain true to this project. The commitment to conduct and guide such inquiry places certain imperative demands on the therapist. The more obvious and objective demands include such items as dependably being on time and alert for sessions, being attentive to what is discussed in the hour, and taking the client seriously. The more subtle demands involve the participation of the therapist's subjectivity.

Freud (1912/1958) broke the ground in this regard when he first discussed the actual technique of psychoanalysis. He suggested that his method

> may be summed up in a single precept [which is] intended to create for the doctor a counterpart to the "fundamental rule of psychoanalysis" which is laid down for the patient [free association]. . . . He must turn his own unconscious like a receptive organ towards the transmitting unconscious of the patient. (pp. 111, 115)

Following this, he must "convert" these tacit impressions into an articulation or interpretation which leads the analysand to "pick up" this same latency. While we no longer use such terms as a therapist's "receptive organ," we continue to follow Freud in insisting that a large part of the therapist's job entails being open to and receptive to the subtle and perhaps hidden stirrings in a client's psyche and to follow such stirrings, even though they may be quite disturbing for the therapist and difficult to tolerate.

While the process of intensive psychotherapy usually necessitates the commitment of both parties to an intimate relationship, the client is in an especially vulnerable position in this relationship. The vulnerability a client brings to therapy or opens to within the course of therapy and which allows for the possibility of change, involves daring to trust in the therapist.

In order to substantively change one's way of being in the world, it is essential that one finds the confidence to surrender to that which one is not. In order to relinquish a way of being that is self-limiting, one must enter into a state of indeterminacy (the unconscious) to face what has appeared faceless and speak what has seemed unspeakable. To accomplish this, which is to engage in life-changing therapy, the client must let go of his or her habitual stance and trust that this letting-go will be contained. Such trust is necessary in order for one to risk the possible dissolution of one's self and to tolerate the vulnerability of unknowing, perhaps even the threat of non-being, with the confidence that the therapist or therapeutic project can contain this emergence. It is from such a state of indeterminacy that it becomes possible to envision or touch into possibilities for a more fruitful way of being. This makes evident that not only is it essential that the client allow him- or herself to become vulnerable to unconscious stirrings, but that the therapist allow him- or herself to tolerate or "hold" unsettled and often disturbing emotional states.

Of course, in order to hold the pathic stirrings of a client's psyche, it is necessary for the therapist to embrace the client's dimension of feeling, since that is what we are entrusted with. However, such intimate contact can be deeply moving in many ways. To the extent that we shy away from making contact and holding an emotional or ideational rawness in a trust, we risk betraying that trust. This can be done passively through withdrawing from confrontation or actively through guiding a client away from a particularly disturbing area which is difficult for us to contain and entertain.

To hold the container is the challenge, and it is not an accomplishment that is done once and forgotten. Instead, it requires a vigilance on the part of the therapist to be true to the felt complexity of an evocative intersubjective field. It is incumbent upon the therapist to confront the palpable otherness within the client and to hold this living being in one's presence.

For example, as Jeff got in touch with deep grief over early childhood woundings, his sadness and the sobs which marked it became a familiar constant of his therapy, which both he and his therapist, Dr. S., came to feel comfortable with. Jeff became more able to identify feelings of powerlessness and dependence on others, including the therapist. In time, his weeping began to give way to grating whining and stifled rage threatening to erupt. This shift marked a period of extreme uneasiness for Dr. S., as Jeff's diffuse anger would occasionally flare into stark hatred directed at the therapist and other significant persons in his life. Upon seeing this dimension of himself, Jeff would be inundated with wrenching guilt and shame. Over a period of some weeks, Dr. S. was challenged with holding a range of volatile and contradictory emotions which he found very evocative. There were numerous occasions where he had to stop himself from berating his client, from objectifying him ("damn narcissist"), and from ignoring his whining plaints.

It would be hubris to suppose that any one of us, as a psychotherapist, will remain forever faithful to a client's process. To assume that we would, or to relax in the false self-assuredness that our observance of formal ethical imperatives will protect us from any lapse, would be folly. Whenever therapy penetrates to levels of subjective meaning, there is the opportunity to be true to that latency or to betray it.

Even when, because of our inexperience, ignorance, or countertransference, we betray the subjective potentiality of a client, this lapse or oversight can still provide more grist for the therapeutic mill. On occasion, betraying a client's process may reveal some truth to that person, especially if the therapist can find the courage to recognize the straying and truly redress the issue. In Jeff's case, one of the therapist's lapses provided just such an opportunity. At one point Dr. S. wound up a session by giving Jeff a mini-lecture on the pitfalls of his spiritual practice. The next session Jeff was furious with Dr. S. for acting as his meditation teacher and assuming such a position of authority over him. As Jeff spoke, Dr. S. sensed the tart taste of humble pie. Jeff had a point: This lecture was misplaced. At the same time, Dr. S. became aware that Jeff's voice had a fullness to it that he had not heard before. As this strength was focused on, Jeff's rage gradually became less diffuse and he became more able to own his power.

Or again, in working with Barbara, the therapist slipped into allowing her to call him any time she felt upset. Eventually, it grew to be too frequent, elicited by too trivial provocations, and too upsetting to the therapist's life. Finally the therapist confronted her and set limits. She felt betrayed. The real betrayal was the therapist's not setting limits earlier and pretending to be all self-sacrificing for her needs.

Rather than linger in an objectifying judgment regarding an incident of therapeutic betrayal, it is possible to attempt to understand the meaning it has for a client. To do so compels the therapist to be true to his or her own subjective receptivity and responsivity, which occurs nowhere else than in the existential, intersubjective moment.

REFERENCES

Bradford, G.K. (1989). Tragedy and the art of questioning in depth psychotherapy. *The Humanistic Psychologist, 17,* 224-250.

Bugental, J.F.T. (1968). Psychotherapy as a source of the therapist's own authenticity and inauthenticity. *VOICES: The Art and Science of Psychotherapy, 4*(2), 13-23.

Bugental, J.F.T. (1978). *Psychotherapy and process: The fundamentals of an existential-humanistic approach.* New York: McGraw-Hill.

Bugental, J.F.T. (1990). *Intimate journeys: Stories from life-changing therapy.* San Francisco: Jossey-Bass.

Freud, S. (1958). Recommendations to physicians practising psycho-analysis. In J. Strachey (Ed. and Trans.), *The standard edition of the complete psychological works of Sigmund Freud* (Vol. 12, pp. 109-120). London: Hogarth Press. (Original work published 1912)

Pope, K. (1988). How clients are harmed by sexual contact with mental health professionals: The syndrome and its prevalence. *Journal of Counseling and Development, 67,* 222-226.

Pope, K. (1990). Therapist-patient sex as sex abuse: Six scientific, professional, and practical dilemmas in addressing victimization and rehabilitation. *Professional Psychology: Research and practice, 21*(4), 227-239.

Rutter, P. (1989). *Sex in the forbidden zone.* Los Angeles: Tarcher.

Living the Symptom

Greg Mogenson

SUMMARY. The problems which psychotherapists are asked to resolve are often the very experiences which the patient should be living. This paper describes how easily the therapist can collude with the patient's rejection of life by agreeing to remove a symptom. After differentiating two therapeutic attitudes, the attitudes of "Merlin" and "Christ," the case of a patient whom the author refused to treat for her "insomnia," lest he collude with her rejection of life, is considered. Finally, Nietzsche's notion of *amor fati* and Tillich's view of courage are examined in terms of their usefulness in therapy.

> My calamity is my Providence.
> Outwardly it is fire and vengeance. Inwardly
> it is light and mercy.
>
> –Baha'u'llah

Symptoms originate in our refusal of them. The penis that won't erect, the vagina that won't open, the black mood that darkens the spirit, the hounding thought that obsesses the mind, the fear that inhibits an initiative: None of these experiences is a *symptom* until we refuse to accept it as a part of life. A sleepless night is just a sleepless night until we attempt to avoid it. A pang of conscience is just a pang of conscience until we flee from it. "Insomnia," "secondary impotence," "vaginismus," "depression," "obsessional think-

Greg Mogenson, MA, is author of *God Is a Trauma: Vicarious Religion and Soul-Making, Greeting the Angels: An Imaginal View of the Mourning Process,* and numerous articles on imagination and psychotherapy. He is in private practice. Mailing address: 135 Edgehill Crescent, London, Ontario. N6G 2T6. Canada.

ing," "anxiety disorders," "neurotic guilt": These "clinical enti-
ties," as well as a host of others, do not exist in their own right, but
rather, are created by our refusal (whether conscious or unconscious) to experience the vicissitudes of life which underpin them.
*Whatever we refuse to suffer as part of life becomes a category of
psychopathology.* The act of saying "No" to life-whether in whole
or in part–calls into being an order of negated existence which
seems, at first, to offer protection from life. But nature abhors a
vacuum. Brush one devil from the house and it returns with seven
more (Matt. 12:44, 45). No sooner do we say no to life than we are
haunted by our unlived life. The mechanism of repression is belied
by the imagination's inability to represent negation. Indeed, it is
precisely our attempt to repress, ward off, or mollify an unwelcome
experience that guarantees that it will pursue us.

Dreams reflect this in striking imagery. Each night we watch
ourselves battling monsters and fleeing the parts of ourselves we
cannot accept. Feelings which we will not allow ourselves to feel
crawl over us like spiders or rats while the dream-ego reaches for
the pesticide can. Enemies threaten and attack us. It is not just that
we see the beam in our brother's eye and not the stick in our own.
It's that the unconscious shows us the face we show it. The frightening events of our dreams, like the unwelcome events of our lives
which they reflect, are a function of our avoidance of them. We are
chased because we are running away.

In family life "pathology" is created in a similar manner. As we
evolve together through time, as our children grow and change, we
often refuse to surrender outmoded strategies of adaptation. The
family as a system tends to lag behind the transitions of its own
life-cycle. New challenges become misconstrued as problems and
are handled anachronistically with tried and true methods that are
already obsolete. The solutions, as the associates of the Mental
Research Institute have so succinctly put it, become the problem
(Watzlawick, Weakland, & Fisch, 1974, pp. 31-39). Little wonder
so many people dread their families and experience the nest as a
place of extinction. To live in the past, rather than in the present, is
not really to live at all.

The refusal of life, like the impassioned living of it, has a
religious quality, albeit a false one. What we refuse to live as part of

life, we reify and deify. The elevator we are afraid to enter, the food we will not allow ourselves to keep down, the house we are unable to leave: Ironically, anything can become sacred in this secular age. Whatever we feel overwhelmed by we propitiate as if it were holy. Whatever we cannot absorb becomes our god.

PATHOLOGY AS RELIGION

The similarity between psychopathology and religion has long been recognized. Freud (1907/1950), in his paper, "Obsessive Acts and Religious Practices," noted the resemblance between the cere- monial behavior of obsessional neurotics and the ritualistic behav- ior which characterizes the religious life. Jung, also, noted this resemblance, although he did not *reduce* religious practices to the pathological syndromes they resembled. "Religions," in Jung's (1964/1970) view, "are psychotherapeutic systems . . . which ex- press the whole range of the psychic problem in mighty images" (p. 172). More recently, archetypal psychologists, among them Hill- man (1975), Giegerich (1988), and Miller (1974), have explored in considerable detail the "divine" backgrounds to a variety of patho- logical conditions. Beginning with Jung's (1967) remark–"the gods have become diseases; Zeus no longer rules Olympus, but rather the solar plexus" (para. 54)–these authors have elaborated a psycholo- gy which is in touch with the religious dimension of our psychic life. My own book, *God Is a Trauma: Vicarious Religion and Soul- Making,* works within this same tradition in its attempt to spell out the religious dimension of a traumatized life (Mogenson, 1989).

Symptoms have a religious quality regardless of whether we have been brought up in a religious tradition or not. So long as we are unwilling to suffer an experience or live our lives to the fullest we are at the mercy of the offended spirits of the life we have not lived. Like a jealous god, the unlived life requires sacrifices–many of them human–to appease its wrath. In earlier ages this was under- stood. In ancient Greece, for instance, long before our current psy- chiatry, a person afflicted with symptoms consulted an oracle in order to find out which god had been offended, which aspect of life had been ignored. Today, however, we don't imagine our lives as a part of a larger order in this same way. Rather than find ways to harmonize ourselves with the flow of life we wish to control that flow.

TECHNOLOGIZED THERAPY

Technology has proven to be a mixed blessing. Not only does it threaten the life of the planet; it tends to dislocate us from our sense of soul. The technological mind has a tendency to turn the problems of life into *technical* problems–forgetting the moral, ethical, religious, and historical dimensions which are also at stake. It is not simply that a little knowledge is a dangerous thing or that fools rush in where angels fear to tread. *The danger is that in exercising our power over life we will fail to empower one another to actually live it.*

These considerations are important for the psychotherapist to consider. The last 30 years have witnessed an unprecedented advance in clinical acumen and technological know-how. Strategic and behavioral therapy, in particular, have contributed a wealth of powerful techniques to the field. How we put this know-how to work–*with what attitude?*–is a crucial issue. In our earnest endeavor to "solve the presenting problem" let us not forget that the presenting problem is also a piece of life. Two wrongs do not make a right–not even paradoxically. If, like the patient, we fail to recognize a symptom's rootedness in life we run the risk of colluding with his or her rejection of that life.

MERLIN AND CHRIST

"If the wrong man uses the right means, the right means work in the wrong way." This Chinese saying, unfortunately only too true, stands in sharp contrast to our belief in the "right" method irrespective of the man who applies it. In reality, everything depends on the man and little or nothing on the method. (Jung, 1967, para. 4)

In Medieval Romance the difference between technical knowhow and the wisdom of life was personified by the figures of Merlin and Christ. Merlin is the technical virtuoso. He has an uncanny knack for making the most obdurate problems of our day-to-day life disappear in thin air. With a turn of a phrase and a pass of his magic wand, this maker of spells can "reframe" a situation such that the problem at its core seems to vanish. Merlin's world is a world of magic and illusion. The assumption that underpins the contemporary version of this wizardry is that we live, move, and have our being in what Watzlawick and others have called an "invented reality." Nothing is sacred. There are no "eternal verities" except those we have fashioned and re-fashioned for ourselves. Anything can be reformulated; everything can be reframed. Abracadabra. Just say "be" and it is.

Christ, on the other hand, is not a magician. Though he is able to perform miraculous healings he does not accomplish this through sorcery. People do not feel tricked by him. He is not an illusionist. On the contrary, he is a teacher who takes the trouble to explain things. His stories and parables contain a practical wisdom and are designed to locate us more congruently in our lives. Though Christ and Merlin both work with metaphors, Christ's metaphors are answerable to life in a way that Merlin's are not. When Merlin utters an incantation or casts a spell he does so in the conviction that his wizardry is better than our real lives. If he brings about change or healing it merely bears witness to his occult powers. Christ's words, on the other hand, are on the side of meaning. This meaning is not something arbitrary which he has brashly invented as part of a brilliant performance. When Christ, the "Living Word," speaks, his words are chosen with the knowledge that one cannot touch a blade of grass without troubling a star. The listener's reality is respected. His goal in speaking is not to exalt himself as a power above all others, but to empower others to more completely inhabit their lives. "I came that you might have life, and might have it abundantly" (1 John 10:10).

Having made this distinction between Merlin and Christ, let me hasten to add that both are necessary. Without the trickery of Merlin, without a sense of our own manipulative power, there is the danger that we may unconsciously enact these very qualities even while we naively think ourselves to be on the side of Christ. As therapists, we must take care that we do not become a party to those priesthoods which, as Blake (1953, p. 127) warned, are established in every age by those few who would turn the poetic tales which heal the soul into forms of worship which enslave it. Parables have a poetic truth, not a literal one, and they must be subverted again and again by Merlin to prevent our therapeutic piety from being reified into a fixed system of salvation. Again, as the Mental Research Institute associates have insisted, our problems are embedded by our dogmatic methods of solving them.

CASE EXAMPLE

During the course of a lengthy, insight-oriented treatment of a young woman whose capacity to attach to her child and to feel adequate as a mother had been severely impeded by her own abusive childhood, I became concerned about the vast number of phobic and obsessional symptoms from which this woman also suffered. Though she exhausted herself each day with the performance of compulsive acts related to housecleaning, and though she suffered a variety of (apparently) inexplicable fears such as a fear of looking out the window, her greatest complaint was insomnia. For 5 years her sleep had been very unsatisfactory, despite the use of various medical interventions. The insomnia question came up one day when I was asking her what she did to comfort herself. I was not enquiring about sleep. I merely wished to know what this woman who had been so massively failed by her earliest caregivers did to take care of herself. One by one she listed off a long list of things she had tried but which she had abandoned. Why, I asked, had she abandoned the pleasure of a bath, the pleasure of reading, the pleasure of an evening walk? As if unaware that any of these things had any value in themselves, she answered that none of them had solved her insomnia. As we continued to pursue this theme it became evident that despite the fact that treating these problems was not a part of our present treatment contract and despite the obvious gains she was making in her relationship to her child, she covertly judged our work together in terms of its lack of impact on her insomnia. At this time I considered making a detour from our previous direction and, donning my strategic-therapy hat, designing an intervention to resolve the insomnia. It would take us off course, but why not contract for a few sessions and free her from her sleeplessness? Or, if I wanted to preserve the current focus, why not subcontract the insomnia for strategic therapy with a colleague? In the end I decided on a third alternative. I decided that I would refuse to treat the insomnia and confront her with her tendency to undervalue our work because it had not met this need.

At our next session I told my patient that I did not want our work–which after all had other goals–to be held answerable to her insomnia. I said that it was unfair to measure her success in therapy and her success in family life with the ruler of insomnia. Neither my support; her increased comfort with being a parent; nor baths, books, or evening walks should be used for the ulterior motive of promoting sleep. As we spoke, a religious metaphor crept into the discourse. I said that she was in a false religion, worshiping a false god. So much in her life–her child, her husband, the therapy, not to mention the multitude of life's simple pleasures–she was sacrificing to the tyrannical God, Insomnia, by rendering them answerable to it. I invited her to accept that a sleepless night was a part of life–something we all suffer. Playing to her sense of dignity, I added that she should stop humiliating herself and adding insult to injury by begging "Mr. Insomnia" to let her sleep with him. "You can sleep with Sleep," I told her, "but not with insomnia." At the conclusion of the session I recommended that she simply give up trying to sleep and start awakening to life by doing things for their own sake instead of turning them into sleeping pills.

My intervention of not intervening proved useful to my patient. Not only has this woman slept better since (there are still some sleepless nights); she has started in other ways to let go of her obsessively controlling stance and to allow life to support and cradle her. She is beginning to bond with the things of her life and no longer holds them at bay in that ambivalent manner which was so characteristic of the way she and her daughter had held each other at bay when I first met them.

DISCUSSION

Of course, my intervention of not intervening was a strategic intervention, well described in the literature (Haley, 1985, p. 59). I had externalized the problem (White, 1988/89; 1990), interdicted my patient's attempted solution (Watzlawick et al., 1974, p. 35), and jammed the "be-spontaneous paradox" (Watzlawick et al., p. 64) in which she had trapped herself, thereby allowing sleep to come unbidden and spontaneously as is its nature and its wont. The subtler point I wish to consider, however, is whether the intervention was in the spirit of magic or miracle, Merlin or Christ. Despite a measure of Merlin's artistry, I think the intervention was clearly intended to empower the patient to live her life more abundantly and was executed in what we have been describing as the more Christic spirit. My metaphors, though they could certainly be described as examples of "re-framing," were in a deeper sense parables. I wasn't trying to trick my patient (except maybe when I said she could sleep with sleep but not with insomnia) or to deceive her. I was trying to supply her with a reading of life that would help her to live it–all of it, including those dark nights of the soul which we today call insomnia. At the same time, I was supplying this woman who felt so failed by the earliest caregivers of her life with a reading of life that would help her to accept my failures as a part of life as well. Had I agreed to treat her insomnia I would have been putting on the robes of a magician. I did not have that much confidence in my wizardry or in wizardry in general. After all, had not everyone else who tried to help her been foiled in their attempts? If I agreed to solve her insomnia not only would I be owning the problem, I would be colluding (however subtly) with that core attitude which underpins so many "symptoms," the attitude of refusing an experience. But, as Hillman (1976) has written, "*Whenever treatment directly neglects the experience as such and hastens to reduce or overcome it, something is being done against the soul.* For experience is the soul's one and only nourishment" (p. 23). More important than "reducing" or "overcoming" the patient's "insomnia," I believed, was helping her to *experience* it. Specifically, the patient needed to experience that a sleepless night was not a bad mother. Were I, through some powerful intervention, to eradicate her tendency to be wakeful at night I would do so at the cost of embedding the split in her representational world, a split which underpinned most, if not all, of her other symptoms, and which it was the purpose of therapy to address. I would become the good mother who brought sleep, but wakeful nights would still be construed as belonging to the domain of the bad mother. In order to integrate good and bad it was crucial for the patient to experience both my helpfulness and my failure to help. Indeed, as Kohut has pointed out, it is not for therapy to successfully provide the patient with what others have failed to provide-that would merely promote infantilization. The therapist must fail the patient as well, though not as massively or abruptly as others have done in the past. It is in this way that the patient internalizes the support that the outer world suddenly ceased to provide (Kohut, 1987, p. 23).

Ironically, Merlin is more apt to play the savior than is Christ. Being on the side of the abundant life, Christ shows us how to live it authentically, even when that entails suffering and crucifixion. "Pick up your cross," he admonishes, "and follow me"(Matt. 16:24). Merlin, on the other hand, can easily fall prey to the power principle. Even when his magic is "white" and he works from the well-intentioned desire to "solve the presenting problem," his magical approach tends to preserve the negative evaluations that the patient has ascribed to those aspects of life he or she has refused to live. As I have expressed it elsewhere, "Whatever we do not face, but gain salvation from, remains unredeemed and becomes Satanic. Evil is the excrement or waste product emitted by the salvation process itself. Ironically, the more we are saved the more there is to be saved from" (Mogenson, 1989, p. 25).

Priesthood, in particular, has tended to turn the empowering Christ of the gospels into an all-powerful Merlin, the cross into a magic wand. Rather than serving as the exemplar of the authentic life, Christ, as vicarious atonement, is now marketed as the antidote for life. Contemporary religious fundamentalism is not a throwback to an earlier age, nor is it a compensation to today's secularism. On the contrary, both are denominations of the same life-refusing religion. Our modern habit of taking sleeping pills and psychotropic medications as if they were the eucharist is utterly consistent with our tendency to view Christ as a pill as well. Indeed, there is precious little difference between the doctor who says, "Take two aspirins and call me in the morning," the therapist who doles out re-frames, and the priest who admonishes his flock to let Jesus suffer their sins and pains for them. All three run the risk of curing the symptom at the expense of the soul, particularly if they discount its importance as a part of life.

Though the work I have described with this patient could be described as a strategic intervention, and though I was aware of the possibility that it might relieve her of her symptom in a paradoxical manner, I was being honest with her in saying that I did not wish to hold our treatment answerable to her complaints about sleepless-ness. I would rather treat her as a soul and wait for healing to come via miracle than to treat her as a machine that might be altered by my magic. In fact, in encouraging her to not let her false god, "Mr. Insomnia," take the measure of the therapy I felt I was wearing a Jungian hat.[1] The religious metaphor was not a strategic attempt to "speak the client's language"–important though this may be. The patient was not a religious woman, at least not in any conscious or collective sense. And yet, her problem was a religious one. Her daily life was full of rituals through which she attempted to propiti-ate the events of life which she refused to honor, suffer and live. I wanted her to have insight into how she was running away from her life. I wanted her to realize that she had been treating herself as a broken thing in need of fixing instead of a soul in need of care. I wanted her to become more open to life. In a later session I shared with her a stanza from D.H. Lawrence's poem, "Healing."

I am not a mechanism, an assembly of various sections.
And it is not because the mechanism is working wrongly,
     that I am ill.
I am ill because of wounds to the soul, to the deep
     emotional self
and the wounds to the soul take a long, long time, only
     time can help
and patience, and a certain difficult repentance
long, difficult repentance, realisation of life's mistake,
     and the freeing oneself
from the endless repetition of the mistake
which mankind at large has chosen to sanctify.
                              (Cited by Hillman, 1976, p. 96.)

AMOR FATI

What patients need to acquire is an attitude toward life which will allow them to live it–all of it, including its more difficult and unpleasant aspects. Somehow they must be encouraged to embrace the calamities and catastrophes inherent in life rather than avoiding them. Part of the difficulty here is that the avoidance of life, as we just heard from D.H. Lawrence, is sanctioned by the collective. Doctors, therapists, and clergy too often play the role of accomplice here. In the name of freeing patients from their symptoms they often intervene in a manner that actually further divorces their patients from life.

The present age is not an age of the exemplary character; it is the age of the tranquilizer. Where once we looked to the example of courageous men and women, now we look to the pharmacist. Our increased capacity to alter our lives, though not in itself a bad thing, has led to a diminution of consciousness. The unpleasant events of life are now so avoidable that we hardly seem to require a philosophy of life. What need have we today of such pharmacologically inert vagaries as wisdom, tenacity, courage, and truth? But so far no cure has been found for death. We will still have to live that last moment of existence–unless our souls have died before the end of our bodily life.

Nietzsche (1967), who, more than any other philosopher, was a philosopher of life, encouraged in his writing an attitude which he called *amor fati:*

> My formula for the greatness of a human being is *amor fati*: that one wants nothing to be different–not forward, not backward, not in all eternity. Not merely bear what is necessary, still less conceal it . . . but *love it.* (p. 258)

The key for Nietzsche to an abundant life is to *"love it."* While the moribund spirit says no to life, the lover of life is a yea-sayer. As lovers of life we do not look away from this existence to other worlds; nor do we look for antidotes beyond the reach of our own creating will. In the affirmation of a single moment we affirm as well all other moments–our childhood, our parents, the accidents of history. Events from the past are redeemed by transforming every

"'It was' into an 'I wanted it thus!'"(Nietzsche, 1961, p. 161). And with the same arms as we embrace ourselves, including "the ugly that could not be removed," we embrace "the fatality of that which has been and will be" saying "Nothing that is may be subtracted, nothing is dispensable" (cited in Kaufmann, 1950, p. 282).

> Did you ever say Yes to one joy? O my friends, then you said yes to *all* woe as well. All things are chained and entwined together, all things are in love;
> if ever you wanted one moment twice, if ever you said: 'You please me, happiness, instant, moment!' then you wanted *everything* to return!
> you wanted everything anew, everything eternal, everything chained, entwined together, everything in love, O that is how you *loved* the world,
> you everlasting men, loved it eternally and for all time: and you say even to woe: 'Go, but return!' *For all joy wants–eternity!* (Nietzsche, 1961, pp. 331-332)

COURAGE

In his book *The Courage To Be* Paul Tillich (1952) suggests that much of what secular psychotherapy would view as pathology and attempt to alleviate or cure, is actually given with life.[2] Anxiety, the threat non-being poses to being, is existential in Tillich's view and only becomes a pathology when we try to escape it. Echoing Jung's clinical observation that within a neurosis is concealed the natural and necessary suffering which the patient has refused to bear, Tillich (1952) writes that "Neurosis is the way of avoiding nonbeing by avoiding being" (p. 66). Rather than collude with their patients' avoidance of being, psychotherapists must en-*courage* them to embrace it. Though we may empathize with their fears, we must not mistake a smaller life for a remedy. The reasonable goal of "solving the presenting problem" degenerates into a moral and spiritual tragedy if the self which is affirmed in the process is a reduced one (Tillich, 1952, p. 66). In order to live life fully courage is required. Indeed, the two stand in a complementary relationship to one another. As Tillich (1952) puts it, "The ontological question of the nature of being can be asked as the ethical question of the nature of courage. Courage can show us what being is, and being can show us what courage is" (p. 2).

Therapy misses the mark when it fails to foster the courage necessary to live the chronicity of life. The symptom-free patient, *soul-lessly desensitized to the threat of nonbeing,* is hardly the ideal toward which therapy should strive, regardless of the fact that this patient is the most impressive from the point of view of an outcome study. Is psychotherapy's "urge to alleviate" a function or symptom of its own lack of the courage to be? Are we therapists perhaps even more uncomfortable with our anxieties than our patients are with theirs? Are they suffering from *our* lack of courage in addition to their own? "Courage," writes Tillich (1952),

> does not remove anxiety. Since anxiety is existential, it cannot be removed. But courage takes the anxiety of nonbeing into itself. Courage is self-affirmation "in spite of," namely in spite of nonbeing. He who acts courageously takes, in his self-affirmation, the anxiety of nonbeing upon himself. . . . Anxiety turns us toward courage, because the other alternative is despair. Courage resists despair by taking anxiety into itself. (p. 2)

In my practice I find that courage can be bolstered. Sometimes I simply ask for it. People know what it is, they just didn't know it was called for. Suddenly, expectations change. They know their anxiety is not going to go away, else the courage wouldn't be called for. In subsequent sessions I celebrate their self-affirming determination, decorate them for their bravery. With other people, the support offered by the therapeutic relationship is enough to enable them to face and suffer what they must. Through empathy we share the anguish and bear it together. Of course, there can be very difficult moments, moments when despair seems to have all but triumphed. Mostly, these seem to correspond to lapses in my own courage. I feel I am not helping, not doing enough. I start thinking of technical procedures and magical interventions. I forget that anxiety, the patient's and my own, is given with life, and that most of it, as Tillich reminds us, will never go away.

NOTES

1. Perhaps the effectiveness of Michael White's (1990, pp. 38-71) technique of externalizing those problems or symptoms which divide patients against themselves or family members against one another resides in its unwitting recognition of the religious manner in which psychic life is actually experienced. In an essay titled, "Psychology and Religion," Jung (1858/1977) writes:

> The truth is that we do not enjoy masterless freedom; we are continually threatened by psychic factors which, in the guise of "natural phenomena," may take possession of us at any moment. The withdrawal of metaphysical projections leaves us almost defenseless in the face of this happening, for we immediately identify with every impulse instead of giving it the name of the "other," which would at least hold it at arm's length and prevent it from storming the citadel of the ego. (p. 87)

White's technique of turning an all-too-personal symptom into an impersonal agency or spirit (a child's encopresis into "sneaky poo") compensates the secularism of our present age. We have lost our supernatural moorings and so must ourselves become the grotesque carriers of the archetypal energies which were once recognized and propitiated as other. Where an earlier age would have automatically attributed their problems to the actions of an existing spirit or deity, we must re-invent the daemons to free us from the perils of identification with them. The point I wish to make is that White's technique is a secularized re-make of yesterday's religion. Perhaps, if we bear this in mind, we can use the technique with the proper, reverential attitude.

2. Though I do not think we can reduce all psychopathology to existential anxiety, I do think that the courage to live in the face of a symptom or a disease is always important. The patient diagnosed with schizophrenia needs more than medicine. He or she needs to be prevented from affirming a smaller identity merely because of the diagnosis.

REFERENCES

Blake, W. (1953). *Selected poetry and prose of Blake*. (Northrope Frye, Ed.). New York: Random House.

Freud, S. (1950). Obsessive acts and religious practises. In E. Jones (Ed.), *Collected papers: vol. II*. London: The Hogarth Press.

Giegerich. W. (1988). *Die atombombe als seelische wirklichkeit. ein versuch uber der geist des christlichen abendlandes*. Zurich: Schweizer Spiegel Verlag, Raben-Reihe.

Haley, J. (1985). *Conversations with Milton H. Erickson, M.D., Vol. One: Changing individuals*. New York: Triangle Press.

Hillman, J. (1975). *Re-visioning psychology.* New York: Harper & Row.
Hillman, J. (1976). *Suicide and the soul.* Dallas: Spring Publications.
Jung, C.G. (1964/1970). The state of psychotherapy today. In *Civilization in transition* (pp. 157-173). Princeton: Princeton University Press.
Jung, C.G. (1967). Commentary on "the secret of the golden flower." In *Alchemical studies* (pp. 1-55). Princeton: Princeton University Press.
Jung, C.G. (1958/1977). Psychology and religion. In *Psychology and religion: east and west* (pp. 4-105). Princeton: Princeton University Press.
Kaufmann, W. (1950). *Nietzsche: philosopher, psychologist, antichrist.* (3rd ed). New York: Random House.
Miller, D. (1974). *The new polytheism.* New York: Harper & Row.
Mogenson, G. (1989). *God is a trauma: Vicarious religion and soul-making.* Dallas: Spring Publications.
Nietzsche, F. (1961). *Thus spoke Zarathustra.* Harmondsworth: Penguin Books.
Nietzsche, F. (1967). *On the genealogy of morals & Ecce home.* New York: Random House.
Tillich, P. (1952). *The courage to be.* New Haven: Yale University Press.
Watzlawick, P., Weakland, J.H., & Fisch, R. (1974). *Change: Principles of problem formation and problem resolution.* New York: W.W. Norton.
White, M. (1988/1989). *Externalizing the problem.* Dulwich Center Newsletter.
White, M., Epston, D. (1990). *Narrative means to therapeutic ends.* New York: W.W. Norton.

The Betrayal of the Child:
The Contributions of Alice Miller

Edward P. Shafranske

SUMMARY. The significance placed on the role of early childhood experience on later development and on the etiology of psychopathology is generally accepted. The trusting relationship of the dependent child to caregivers is frequently violated in many ways and may be viewed as constituting a betrayal of the child. This article presents the contributions of Alice Miller, a psychoanalyst by training, who has, through her published work, brought international attention to the abuse of children.

The infant comes into the world endowed with a biologically rooted imperative to forge relationships with others. Through an inherent propensity for attachment, the child insures and actively shapes the ministrations of those upon whom he or she depends (Bowlby, 1969). Further, the child intuits a sense of self and gleans the nature of human existence through myriad encounters with others, most particularly, those engagements with mother and father. The child's physical well-being and psychological health are therefore entrusted to the parents. In addition, the child's construction of the meaning of self and others is cultured within the family and forms the bedrock upon which later development occurs. Bollas (1987) commented that within the caregiving relationship an "aesthetic of care" is communicated by the parents and serves as the basis for the child's "aesthetic of being." This thesis suggests that the manner in which children are attended to and related with sets

Edward P. Shafranske, PhD, is on the faculty of the Graduate School of Education and Psychology of Pepperdine University, Pepperdine University Pl., 400 Corporate Pointe, Culver City, CA 90230.

27

the tone for their own appreciation of themselves and respect that they will accord to their existence as persons throughout their lives. This is in keeping with Kohut's and others' claims that a person's foundational sense of self and others, in consort with the regulation of esteem, is established within the primary relationships of childhood (Kohut, 1971, 1977; Lichtenberg, 1975; Stern, 1985). It is not surprising, therefore, the significance we place on the role of early childhood experience on later development and on the etiology of psychopathology.

The child's passive dependence is balanced, in part, through the child's active readiness for attachment and on his or her budding capabilities for both alloplastic and autoplastic adaptivity. The child's desire for relationship and struggling attempts at adaptation convey what seems to be a natural proclivity to contribute to a trusting, cooperative relationship with one's caregivers. In the best of circumstances, parents and child honor this trusting relationship throughout the progressions and regressions which make up the course of maturation. There are, however, instances in which the trusting relationship is violated. These violations go beyond the vicissitudes of separation-individuation or other developmental challenges, and may be viewed as constituting a betrayal of the child. From blatant cases of physical and sexual abuse to less obvious violations of trust, children are betrayed by those figures in whom dependency and faith have been entrusted.

The effects of childhood abuse and deprivation as manifested in psychopathology and criminality are well reported within the annals of the social sciences. My intent is not to summarize this voluminous literature but rather to present the contributions of one individual who has spoken out stridently on the betrayal of children. Alice Miller, a psychoanalyst by training, in a series of works published over the past 10 years, has brought international attention to the abuse of children, the psychological dynamics involved in the cycle of abuse, the "poisonous pedagogy" of certain child-rearing practices, and a critique of psychoanalytic treatment. The following works, available in English, will provide the basis for our discussion of betrayal: *The Drama of the Gifted Child* (Miller, 1981), *For Your Own Good* (Miller, 1983), *Thou Shalt Not Be Aware: Society's*

Betrayal of the Child (Miller, 1984), *The Untouched Key* (Miller, 1990a), and *Banished Knowledge* (Miller, 1990b).

THE BETRAYAL OF THE CHILD

Through the mirroring responses of the mother the child comes to experience the nuances of his or her own drives and affects which color and give vitality to nascent self-representations. Contained within the mirroring responses are the mothers' implicit valuations of the child's existence.

If we start from the premise that a person's whole development (and his narcissistic balance that is based upon it) is dependent on the way *his mother* experienced *his expression of needs and sensations* during his first days and weeks of life, then we must assume that here the *valuation of feelings* and *impulses* is set. (Miller, 1981, p. 84)

To the extent that the mother accepts and delights in the reality of the child's states of being, the young person is set on a path of self-acceptance and integrity. In the setting in which the mother is more invested in her projections or who the baby should be, a course is primed in which the child will devalue his or her subjective sense of self and attenuate to the limits of the parent's narcissistic expectations. The child is betrayed in the parents' unspoken demand to be other than who he or she is; a budding "false self" begins to take form in the shadow of the parents' expectations. Miller (1983) points out that "the malleability of the sensitive child is nearly boundless, permitting all the parental demands to be absorbed by the psyche" (p. 258). Reflecting the contributions of Kohut (1971, 1977) and Winnicott (1965), Miller stresses the long-standing, harmful effects of the child's adaptation to the parents' narcissistic projections. The child, suffering from an inevitable narcissistic disorder, matures alienated from his or her authentic needs and feelings. Within the constraints of a false sense of self, such a person locates direction not from within the truth of one's drives, affects, and aspirations but rather from the introjected expectations of others. To understand the nature of this early betrayal requires a sensitivity to the "subjective experience of being ignored, the narcissistic wounding and humiliation of the child [that] can be measured fully only if narcissistic needs for respect, acceptance, and being taken seriously are given due consideration along with [the child's] physical needs" (Miller, 1984, p. 62). Such a betrayal of children leads to the inwardly empty sense of self, interpersonal alienation, and vapid directionlessness and anomie which express the narcissistic sufferings of many adults. Their emotional scars are revealed only in their desperate attempts to assuage the dictates of introjects and their craving for psychic substance to fill their inner void. In the striving for achievement and external status, the narcissistically injured may express contempt for the aspects of the child within: weakness, impotence, uncertainty, and the pangs of loneliness (Miller, 1982, p. 103). It is in the critical moments in treatment when such a patient can face

the emotional insight that all the love he has captured with so much effort and self-denial was not meant for him as he really was, that the admiration for his beauty and achievements was aimed at this beauty and these achievements, and not at the child himself. In analysis, the small and lonely child asks: "What would have happened if I had appeared before you, bad, ugly, angry, jealous, lazy, dirty, smelly? Where would your love have been then? And I was all those things as well. Does this mean that it was not really me whom you loved, but only what I pretended to be? The well-behaved, reliable, empathic, understanding and convenient child, who in fact was never a child at all? What became of my childhood? Have I not been cheated out of it? I can never return to it. I can never make up for it. From the beginning I have been a little adult. My abilities-were they simply misused?" (Miller, 1981, p. 15)

Such is the consequence of a lifelong devaluation of the real and the betrayal of the authentic expression of the self.

POISONOUS PEDAGOGY

Miller suggests that, in addition to the range of narcissistic injuries, children are assaulted, as well, through what she terms "poisonous pedagogy" which is expressed through certain culturally proscribed attitudes and practices of child-rearing. At the heart of these attitudes and practices is the demand for the renunciation and control of impulses and the production of "good behavior." She cites a 19th-century educational text as illustrative of the deep structure of our attitudes toward children's impulse life:

Therefore, [God's] love is concerned that the child learn at an early age to renounce, control, and master himself, that he not blindly follow the promptings of the flesh and the senses but rather the higher will and the promptings of the spirit . . . it knows also how to bring good by causing hurt, it can impose harsh renunciation, like a physician who prescribes bitter medicine. (Miller, 1983, p. 29)

Such an attitude fosters a justification for all forms of abuse of children in the name of their own good. Parents may exact harsh punishment on children for the sake of instilling within them self-discipline. In Miller's view, such practices not only do not foster a healthy regard and expression of one's drives but in fact engender a primitive splitting of ego states and poor integration of somatic needs and modes of expression. She calls not for a permissive approach for that would simply be a reactionary response which remains embedded in the pedagogical. Nor does she espouse a call for morality or the performance of duty, which she views as "artificial measures that become necessary when something is missing" (Miller, 1983, p. 85). Rather, she suggests that

Children who are respected learn respect. Children who are cared for learn to care for those weaker than themselves. Children who are loved for what they are cannot learn intolerance. In an environment such as this they will develop their *own* ideals, which can be nothing other than the humane, since they grow out of the experience of love. (Miller, 1984, p. 97)

Children who have been denied their feelings and needs and who have recoiled from the sting of a poisonous pedagogy in which violence and humiliation are masked as disciplinary measures for the child's own good have profound difficulty discovering the humane. A consequence of the betrayal with which they suffered is that personal actions are not founded on a sensitivity to human vicissitudes but rather are established in response to a harsh pedagogy which teaches little about human dignity, consideration, and compassion. Further, as parents such persons are disquieted by the vitality which is evidence in their children; they have little compassion for the varied expressions of humanness and attempt "to prevent those qualities that were once scorned and eradicated in [themselves] coming to life in [their] children (Miller, 1983, p. 90). Miller concludes,

> If parents have had to learn very early in life to ignore their feelings, not to take them seriously, to scorn or ridicule them, they will lack the sensitivity required to deal sensitively with their children. As a result, they will try to substitute pedagogical principles as prostheses. (p. 98)

THE CYCLE OF BETRAYAL

Beyond such conflicts lies an equally troubling effect: the buildup of aggression which results from the infliction of cruelty in the name of pedagogy. The child not only learns to distrust and to inappropriately attend to drive states but also feels rage toward the figures to whom he or she is most attached. In that this aggression is engendered toward those to whom the child is abjectly dependent and utterly powerless, the primitive rage is split off from consciousness and denied expression. Through repression and a host of other defensive maneuvers the aggression remains unmetabolized (cf. Kernberg, 1975, 1984) as if awaiting an opportunity for expression and mastery. Herein lies the epigenesis of aggression and human destructiveness.

Miller (1981, 1983, 1984, 1990a, 1990b), through a series of psychohistorical essays and case studies, posits that this anger does not disappear, "but is transformed with time into a more or less conscious hatred directed against either the self or substitute persons, a hatred that will seek to discharge itself in various ways permissible and suitable for an adult" (1983, p. 61). The cycle of abuse and betrayal is thus established as such hatred finds expression within the permissible parameters of poisonous pedagogy or within heinous crimes committed upon society.

When the abused child, now as parent, is again confronted with the helpless and disowned child of the past in his or her progeny, the welled-up aggression finds an outlet for discharge. Through the often clinically noted repetition compulsion, the aggression of the past is meted out upon the displacement figure. As in sadism, the victim becomes the aggressor in an attempt to master the past abuse. Further, as the parent faces his or her lack of omnipotent control of the child (which the parental introjects demand), frustration and a desperate sense of incompetence is rekindled once again within the individual. Faced with the return of the repressed, the child, now as powerful parent, discharges and displaces the rage onto the "unruly" child. Through the exercise of force and physical abuse the parent may strike out in vain attempts to restore his or her "narcissistic equilibrium" (Miller, 1983, p. 162). If corporal punishment was accepted as "a necessary measure" for one's "bad" behavior, then so too will be the fate of the children. The function of the displacement is concealed through the legitimacy poisonous pedagogy provides.

The rage of the child finds its expression as well within other acts of human destruction within society at large. Miller suggests that such was the case of Adolph Hitler. Through her reading of biographical texts she concludes that Hitler was abused and humiliated as a child. The expression of his rage was not contained within a family of his own but rather was displaced onto a whole people, the Jews and others, through splitting and projection. The case of Hitler provides one answer to the question, "What takes place in a child who is humiliated and demeaned by his parents on the one hand and on the other is commanded to respect and to love those who treat him in this fashion and under no circumstances give expression to his suffering?" (Miller, 1983, p. 145). The response lies in a fateful reenactment, in Hitler's case, on a scale almost unimaginable, in which the child who was persecuted becomes the persecutor. Where he had to endure humiliation in silence, now others would cringe under his gaze; where he was once powerless, now others were made subordinate to his will; where he experienced "soul murder," others were exterminated. Miller (1983) suggests that "through the agency of his unconscious repetition compulsion, Hitler actually succeeded in transferring the trauma of his family life onto the entire German nation" (p. 161). The atrocities for which Hitler is solely responsible illustrate the power and the tragedy of such repetition compulsion in which the cycle of abuse may be expressed in such heinous form.

Aggression is not the sole component within the repetition compulsion. For persons with narcissistic vulnerabilities the needfulness within the caregiving relationship and poor attunement are reenacted within the mothering dyads. As narcissistic individuals determine to be perfect parents the cycle of betrayal repeats. Miller (1983) writes:

> The attempt to be the ideal parent, that is, to behave correctly toward the child, to raise her correctly, not to give too little or too much, is an attempt to be the ideal child-well behaved and dutiful-of one's own parents. But as a result of these efforts the needs of the child go unnoticed. I cannot listen to my child with empathy if I am inwardly preoccupied with being a good mother. (pp. 257-258)

Further, whatever attitudes and procedures of one's parents which were utilized to break the spirit of the child may return as the parent-child confronts the vitality of his or her son or daughter. "If it was never possible for us to relive on a conscious level the rejection we experienced in our own childhood and to work it through, then we in turn will pass this rejection on to our children" (Miller, 1983 pp. 3-4).

The linchpin in the cycle of abuse does not lie solely in the repetition of specific acts of abuse but rather rests in the person's conscious recognition and working through of the feelings associated with the history of abuse. Through psychological treatment the reality of abuse may be experienced and the cycle of betrayal broken. When parents discover the history of their own abuse they may be enlightened to the dynamic underpinnings upon which their child-rearing practices are based. "There will surely also be some change in parents' behavior when they learn that what they have previously practiced in good faith as 'necessary disciplining' is in reality a history of humiliating, hurting, and mistreating the child" (Miller 1983, p. 206). Our discussion now turns to the role of psychotherapy in addressing the betrayal of the child.

PSYCHOTHERAPY

The opportunity which psychotherapy affords the patient might simply be put as "the permission to know" (Miller, 1983, pp. 271-279). The praxis of Miller's therapeutic approach concerns the seeing through the repetition compulsion, in which the abuse is reenacted, to the original state of relations between the child and parents. By this she refers less to a biographical search for one specific, life-turning event than to a recovery of the overarching affective and behavioral tone which permeated the relationship of the patient with his or her parents.

She places emphasis on the development of insight and working through of affective and impulse-laden material. "Changes in personality occurring during analysis do not stem from 'corrective emotional experiences' but from insights the patient arrives at by repetition, remembering, and working through relevant material" (Miller, 1984, p. 52). To continue in her words:

The healing process begins when the once absent, repressed reactions to traumatization (such as anxiety, rage, anger, despair, dismay, pain, grief) can be articulated in analysis; then the symptoms, whose function it had been to express the unconscious trauma in a disguised, alienated language incomprehensible both to the patient and those around him, disappear. (p. 53)

Through the empathic presence of the psychotherapist, utilizing the skills of clarification and interpretation, the hitherto banished knowledge of the trauma comes to light. Miller suggests that the

psychotherapist may first garner a sense of the inner child's suffering through the manner in which the patient receives affective experience within the clinical setting. The patient may distrust, disown,
ridicule, or abuse himself or herself for his or her feelings. Further,
within transference phenomena, the early traumatization and the
child's reactions are reenacted within the therapeutic relationship.
Miller views such reenactment from the perspective of the child and
with the belief that the productions are the expressions of actual
trauma. She parts company with and is highly critical of Freudian
psychoanalysis which may approach such production with skepti-
cism and denial, viewing such memories as amalgams of the patient's unexpressed oedipal wishes and conflicts. Miller (1984)
comments, "I *always* regard myself as the advocate of the child in
my patients; whatever they may tell me, I take their side completely
and identify fully with the child in them who is usually not yet able
to express his feelings and delegates them to me" (p. 59).

To take the side of the child involves not only technical skill but
more fundamentally requires that the psychotherapist have empathy
for his or own self in whatever suffering and humiliation was endured in childhood. If the psychotherapist has not worked through
the poisonous pedagogy of his or her own past then he or she will
produce within the therapy the same defensive maneuvers, denial,
and repression which kept the acknowledgment of the truth from
occurring. In such a circumstance, the patient will not be given
permission to know the truth and to fully express the feelings
associated with the traumatization. Rather, the psychotherapist, in
collusion with the parents (his or her own and those of the patient),
will demand understanding of the parents' position and a denial of
the child's experience.

Miller's critique of Freudian metapsychology suggests that
Freud's rejection of his early discoveries of child abuse and the
subsequent development of drive theory stemmed from his inability
to come to grips with his own childhood humiliations (see Masson,
1984). Miller asserts that Freudian psychoanalysis contributes to
poisonous pedagogy through shielding the parents, concealing trauma, and through the application of drive theory in which the responsibility for the trauma or fantasized trauma finds its origin in the
libidinal wishes of the child. In such an instance, the patient's expe-

rience is once again dismissed and the appeal of the child for understanding and acceptance is betrayed.

If on the other hand past traumas have been acknowledged and worked through, then the psychotherapist is enabled "to empathize with what a child is feeling when he or she is defenseless, hurt, or humiliated [like] suddenly seeing in a mirror the suffering of one's own childhood" (Miller, 1983, p. 177). "If the analyst has seen for himself that *his* rage did not kill his parents, he will no longer feel compelled to protect the patient's parents from rage by working towards reconciliation" (Miller, 1984, p. 60). In such a clinical setting, the empathic response of the psychotherapist provides the assistance that encourages the patient to acknowledge the truth and to express the associated pain, rage, disappointment, and loneliness.

In the treatment process the patient may experience a range of reactions to the discovery of childhood abuse. The patient works through the feelings of rage, disappointment, and loneliness as he or she recovers the child of the past and views in new light the adult who one has become. Miller (1984) writes:

At first the patient suffers greatly from the discovery that he has been conforming all his life for the sake of what has turned out to be merely the illusion of concern for him on the part of others. Once it becomes clear to him that he has been clinging to the smiling masks of others, he realizes the extent of his loneliness. Now that the masks have been removed on both sides, he no longer has to make an effort to behave as expected and gains more and more freedom as a result. (p. 86)

With newfound empathy, the patient may face the ways in which he or she was treated as a child, "contemptuously, derisively, disapprovingly, seductively, or by making him feel guilty, ashamed, or frightened" (Miller, 1984, p. 12). "The experience of one's own truth, and the postambivalent knowledge of it, makes it possible to return to one's world of feelings at an adult level–without paradise, but with the ability to mourn (Miller, 1981, p. 15). Through the working-through process the patient integrates the pain of the past, and having recovered and expressed his or her feelings is enabled to break the cycle of betrayal. As rage turns to sorrow the need for the expression and displacement of aggression draws to a final close. Through the conscious acknowledgment and expression of affect the trauma is directly experienced and no longer needs to be expressed within the repetition compulsion. As Miller (1984) writes,

[If] feelings associated with the child's first attachment figures can be *experienced,* they will no longer need to be abreacted in the repetition compulsion with substitute objects. Paradoxical as it may sound, if the impotent hatred of early childhood can be experienced, destructive and self-destructive behavior will come to an end. (p. 175)

The outcome of the therapeutic process is the working through of childhood traumata and, in Miller's view, does not include the adult patient's reconciliation with his or her still-living parents. To include such a reconciliation on the therapeutic agenda would be to introduce a pedagogical dictate to the patient. To make such an implicit demand to forgive and to reconcile with one's parents repeats the disregard that the patient experienced within the trauma. By working through the internalized parental introjects and past traumata the patient is afforded a clearer view of the nature of past and present relationships. Through the increase in freedom and personal autonomy, accomplished through psychotherapy, the patient will be in a position to determine the nature of the resolution and relationship with his or her parents which best addresses his or her interests. Miller (1984) comments:

To be reconciled with these parents does not mean to beg their forgiveness on bended knee, like the Prodigal Son; it merely means to find out what one's parents were like (ones' own parents and not one's siblings') and to accept this fact. Such an acceptance is part of the mourning process and is thus connected with the patient's emotional awakening to the reality of his childhood. (p. 207)

Having become familiar with the parental introjects, more fully mindful of who his or her parents were in the past and are in the present, and freed from the dictates of pedagogy and the repetition compulsion, the patient is more fully prepared to live in the world sensitive to his or her needs, feelings, and aspirations.

CONCLUSION

Miller challenges psychotherapists to be aware of the suffering of children, to be mindful that within all patients, regardless of the nature and expression of their psychopathology, lies the trauma of betrayal. Her work suggests, as well, that "it is only through the (limited) acquaintance with [our] own unconscious [life] and the recognition of the repetition compulsion that makes it possible for [psychotherapists] to understand the subjectivity of another person" (Miller, 1984, p. 8). Furthermore, psychotherapists' sensitivity to the suffering of others will be delimited by their ability to accept their own suffering as persons. And lastly, Miller draws attention to the role of psychological theories which, as systems of abstraction, serve either to assist in the discovery of truth, or as vehicles of pedagogy, serve to dismiss or obfuscate the lived experience of the other. As Miller has pointed out, psychotherapy offers both the potential for the healing of betrayal or, in the hands of pedagogues, its continuation.

REFERENCES

Bollas, C. (1987). *The shadow of the object.* New York: Columbia University Press.
Bowlby, J. (1969). *Attachment and loss* (Vol. I. *Attachment*). New York: Basic Books.
Kernberg, O.F. (1975). *Borderline conditions and pathological narcissism.* New York: Jason Aronson.
Kernberg, O.F. (1984). *Severe personality disorders: Psychotherapeutic strategies.* New Haven: Yale University Press.
Kohut, H. (1971). *The analysis of the self: A systematic approach to the psychoanalytic treatment of narcissistic personality disorders.* New York: International Universities Press.
Kohut, H. (1977). *The restoration of the self.* New York: International Universities Press.

Lichtenberg, J.D. (1975). The development of a sense of self. *Journal of the American Psychoanalytic Association, 23*, 453-461.

Masson, J. (1984). *Assault on truth: Freud's suppression of the seduction theory.* New York: Farrar, Strauss and Giroux.

Miller, A. (1983). *For your own good* (H. & H. Hannum, Trans.). New York: Farrar, Strauss and Giroux.

Miller, A. (1984). *Thou shalt not be aware: Society's betrayal of the child* (H. & H. Hannum, Trans.). New York: New American Library.

Miller, A. (1990a). *Banished knowledge* (H. & H. Hannum, Trans.). New York: Doubleday.

Miller, A. (1990b). *The drama of the gifted child* (R. Ward, Trans.). New York: Basic Books. (Original work published 1981)

Miller, A. (1990c). *The untouched key* (H. & H. Hannum, Trans.). New York: Doubleday.

Stern, D.N. (1985). *The interpersonal world of the infant.* New York: Basic Books.

Winnicott, D.W. (1965). *The maturational processes and the facilitating environment.* New York: International Universities Press.

Betrayal:
A Major Psychological Problem
of Our Time

Louis Birner

SUMMARY. Betrayal in all its forms has been and is an ever-present reality in every area of life: politics, business, human relationships, and so on. However, the psychology of betrayal has not received much attention. This paper will try to shed some light on the psychological issues behind why some of us have an unconscious need to be betrayed or to betray another. Case examples are presented.

It is amazing to consider the fact that the psychology of betrayal has received so little public interest and attention in our frequently corrupt and rather dishonest world. Almost daily we read in newspapers about horrible acts of betrayal in the varied forms of crimes of incest, child abuse, the bribing of judges, actions of crooked lawyers, bought-off senators and representatives, and thieving bankers who embezzle their unfortunate depositors' funds by the millions. The terrible event of the betrayal of another's trust can be found anywhere. In the corporate world it is not uncommon to hear of gross misrepresentations, double dealings, price fixings, various forms of cheating, the callous lack of concern of management for the care and welfare of their employees and of our environment.

Louis Birner, PhD, is a member of the National Psychological Association for Psychoanalysis. He is in the private practice of psychoanalysis and group therapy. He has done work in the areas of problems of procrastination and writer's block and has produced audiocassette tapes dealing with these problems. Mailing address: 823 Park Ave., New York, NY 10021.

41

National and international betrayals are common events. Nations break treaties they once swore on all that is holy to honor and uphold. Political groups have been known to kidnap, abuse, and kill innocent hostages. Nations can attack each other and destroy the enemy's territory and kill innocent citizens for no real or moral reason. Often a warring nation will justify killing thousands of civilians by saying it is "bringing freedom to all."

One sadly notes that such terrible actions of treachery, deceit, and betrayal are in reality commonplace events; however, the psychological motivations for these terrible acts are rarely studied. This paper will try to shed some light on the psychological issues behind why some of us have an unconscious need to be betrayed or to betray another. A review of world history from Adam and Eve on clearly indicates that there is a psychological potential for nations, groups, and people to commit acts of betrayal.

In this discussion betrayal will be defined as

1. an act calculated to lead another person astray;
2. an act of deception or treachery;
3. a breach of confidence or trust.

The betrayer, in some form or other, works to hurt and injure the betrayed party. The tendency to commit acts of betrayal is based on an unconscious process that is learned in childhood; it is a kind of emotional interaction that starts when mothers or fathers cannot adequately fulfill their caretaking roles. When parents do not provide an appropriate amount of love, interest, and caring and engage in acts of neglect, cruelty, sadism, drug addiction, and so on, they deceive, mislead, and misuse their children and dishonor the role and promise of parenthood. This kind of parenting is betrayal itself. Such parents do not help their children to grow, develop, or nurture their talents; they make a mockery of the very promise of their children's future.

Psychologists often speak of the development of "capacity." Winnicott (1965) talks of a maturational environment that can lead the child to develop those capacities necessary for growth, learning, and personal fulfillment. When the early emotional environment is destructive, the child's moral sense is perverted and "reality" becomes an issue of who is to be injured next. The development of positive moral values has little chance in a toxic family situation, especially for the growing youngster. Sad to say, but many people come from homes where a sense of honor and trust is a liability. When parents betray the role of parenthood by being hurtful to their offspring, not only do they injure their own but they serve as an actual model and example for the child in terms of "how to" betray, hurt, or deceive another person. Parents who lie also unwittingly train their child in the practice of lying. Those who hit or sexually abuse their own literally prepare their children to become part of a new generation of child molesters and sexual perverts. Recent research (Shengold, 1985) has indicated that most of the parents who sexually abuse their children were as children sexually misused themselves. The sins of the parents tend to be handed down from generation to generation. Youngsters who have been significantly betrayed emotionally, in any form, are psychologically programmed early on in the practice of betraying other people; and such behavior can become a compulsive ritual. Indeed, when they come to adulthood they have had much firsthand experience in some form of treachery, deceit, and deception.

Children who have been betrayed were psychologically set up to later play out the role of a victim. This is especially true if, after having received abuse, the child was then given some token of reward or caring. In these cases it is easy for the youngster to reason that with enough insult and hurt from the parent there will come a reward of love and caring. When the child believes that by enduring enough pain and devaluation he or she will find love, the need to become a victim is created. This type of person always looks to reproduce the original betrayal that was once experienced at the hands of the parents. Abusers are sought after in the hope of finding love.

Shengold (1985) notes that in the act of "soul murder" the capacity to love, have a love life or an instinct for love is destroyed. In place of the ability to love, the child may learn to value hatred, abuse, and the torture of the other. He notes that in one of the great cases of psychoanalysis, that of Dr. Schreber, the poor man describes himself as having his soul murdered and wrote that his sexuality and identity were taken away from him. In his paranoid delusion he became the bride of God.

Dr. Schreber was "scientifically" raised by his father and was grossly abused and battered in the name of "modern child rearing." There is no doubt that this poor man was later driven to a psychotic state by this cruel treatment. In this case the evil father made his son a victim of his madness to produce a "healthy child." Such treachery in the name of caring is not unusual.

History has produced a number of infamous people who, when they gained political leadership, deceived and betrayed their nation, people, moral principles, and God. Every country has a series of heroes and traitors in its past. Traitors and betrayers are to be found in the Old and New Testaments, in myth and literature, in the fields of art and science, in government and labor unions, and so on. Marriage sometimes ends in anger and disappointment as a result of treachery and deceit on the part of one or both of the mates. People who constantly try to hurt and betray the other person exist at all ages and places and in all walks of life.

History has sadly recorded acts of world leaders and political movements that have tragically betrayed the most common decent human values and humanity itself. Consider that horrible institution of slavery, an evil practice that exploited and destroyed people on the basis of the color of their skin. Genocide, another horror, was based on the insane idea that it was a way of "purifying a race" and making "a better world." The mad leaders of our time pervert humanity by their oppressive and psychotic behavior. Hitler and Stalin used any excuse to kill and torture those people who did not agree with them. They created the work camp and the concentration camp, and the Germans invented and used the gas chamber as a "final solution." These madmen betrayed their own people and humanity at large as they institutionalized killing innocent human beings by the millions.

The potential to be betrayed also exists in all forms of professional relationships. It is quite common to hear people say that they were deceived or mistreated by their doctor or lawyer. Two of the most vulgar expressions in the English language are synonyms for betrayal: "I got fucked," or "I got screwed" usually refer to someone who experienced an act of deception. In everyone's background are episodes of being betrayed at least once.

The legend of Oedipus Rex is a tale of hatred and betrayal.

Oedipus was conceived as a result of a deception and seduction. Jocasta got Laius drunk in order to get pregnant. Laius, the father, did not want the child and tried to kill his son as soon as he was born because he feared the prediction that one day this child would kill him. Tragically, he creates his own murderer and years later he is indeed killed by his own son, who is then unaware that this man is his father. All of the principals in this universal drama deceive and betray the other, thus arranging their own tragic ends.

In many industries fraudulent practices are common events. In the eighties a number of major and minor stock-brokerage houses practiced major fraud and deception on an unsuspecting public. Of course, we have all read about the fabulous profits that the "inside traders" made through these dishonest activities. Telephone fraud is a common practice and very smooth con men can call and tell you that you have to buy a certain stock, bargain, or article. They promise all sorts of rewards if you send them a check. The number of dishonest schemes to separate a person from his or her money are endless.

All neurosis and psychosis involves the person in the experience of betrayal. Mental disturbance is the work of treachery. The extent and degree of betrayal that one experiences in the early developmental years helps to set the psychological stage for later emotional problems. Paranoids and psychotics are victims of an extreme degree of betrayal in their very early years. They have been so hurt and abused in their childhood development that they feel there is no one left in this world for them to trust. Everyone who walks into a psychotherapist's office is a victim of some degree of hurt, abuse, and betrayal.

People who betray others are also found practicing in the professions of psychotherapy and psychoanalysis. A degree or a license in any professional field is no guarantee of ability, sanity, purity, or honesty on the part of the practitioner.

In the mental health field a paradox exists on both sides of the couch. Many people come to psychotherapy with the best of intentions; however, on a deeper level they do not want to get better and, unwittingly, they try to defeat the process of therapy. This desire to destroy or defeat the treatment is not a conscious thing, it is more an unconscious repetition of an earlier history of self-hurt and self-deception, a kind of unhappy drama that tends to be played over and over again. Some of us were well trained in "how to" look for and find disappointment, hurt, and dissatisfaction in our dealings with others. When some of us want to get something that is good and positive there often is a mental counterforce in operation to arrange for us to find disappointment. People with this need to experience betrayal tend to sabotage the treatment in one way or another. Children who have not been loved enough tend to hate, and the need to "kill the other off" can become a part of the personality structure (Klein, 1977).

Now, if there are patients who do not want to get better, there are also many professionals who unwittingly and unconsciously work to defeat the treatment process. They tend to resist helping the patient get better because of the effects of their own inner conflicts. Finell (1985) notes that the narcissism of the analyst makes the patient a victim of the "Doctor's" self-centeredness. These conflicts unexpectedly and subtly intrude themselves into the treatment situation. What makes betrayal such a complicated powerful issue in the therapeutic situation is that people are not aware of their neurotic actions and self-deceptions until they are suddenly confronted by some huge and unexpected disappointment. Sometimes in the process of therapy unconscious motives can push either the therapist or the patient to violate the mutual trust that should be a constant part of the treatment situation.

Three short cases will be presented which deal with some of the aspects of the problem of betrayal and its role as a resistance in the treatment situation.

WALT

Although born into a very wealthy home, Walt was the product of a very deprived and emotionally troubled background. He was brought up by a very abusive mother and a mostly absent, passive, businessman father. The patient described his mother as a terrible sadist, a hitter, a screamer, and a punisher. The main target for all of her irrational anger and aggression was her only son. His early life at home was a nightmare and a disaster. As a child he was an introvert and given to spending long hours by himself studying. If he did his homework, stayed in his room, and did not make noise, the mother would leave him there in peace. As a youngster he was somehow able to find comfort in being by himself and he never learned to trust to get close to anyone at all. Later on, Walt gained some recognition and satisfaction by doing well at school and becoming an excellent student.

Walt grew up a loner and when he reached adolescence did not socialize with his peers. He always did well in intellectual areas and at college was considered an outstanding student. When he finished his undergraduate work he went on to law school and, after graduating, established himself as a very successful lawyer. Anything that demanded the use of his mind came easily to him. But situations that required him to get friendly or emotionally close with another person scared him. As a young man in his middle twenties he was much afraid of women and sexuality.

One day he told a colleague at his law office about his social and sexual fears. The friend suggested that perhaps he would become less frightened of women and of his sexuality if he received some psychological counseling. This friend referred Walt to me for psychotherapy. When I first saw him I was struck by his appearance; he was a very good-looking, tall, extremely well-dressed person and most polite in his speech and manner. Whatever his true feelings were, it seemed that he kept them under very tight wraps. There was a certain rigidity about him and his language was proper, logical, and correct, without humor or emotion. No feelings or humor came through at all when he spoke about himself or his life.

Walt informed me that he wanted to be free of his sexual fears and to feel comfortable in the company of women. When he spoke he almost sounded like a teacher; and my assignment (according to the patient) was to find out why he was so afraid of women and to help him become free of his problem so that he could have sexual intercourse. I felt during that first session that I was being treated like an auto mechanic as he told me about all the things that he wanted to have fixed. I made the observation that Walt seemed to be very removed from me, from his true feelings, and from humanity in general.

For all of his initial resistances and rigidity, Walt worked hard at therapy and followed the rules of treatment. In a few years time he had made some very significant gains, began to feel a bit more relaxed and comfortable with women, and even managed to let himself have sexual intercourse with a woman he had known for some time. His life appeared better and he was achieving some of his treatment goals.

One day, after 3 years of analysis, he suddenly began to remember some of the very traumatic scenes of his early childhood. His mother, who was probably psychotic, would beat him, then lock him in his room and let him cry himself to sleep. He recalled his fear, hurt, and disappointment over this terribly sadistic behavior. He then began to recall the sad fact that his father actually permitted the mother to be so cruel and abusive to him and never, ever defended him or tried to change his grim childhood situation or take him away from his cruel mother. The father just did not care for his welfare.

As Walt would recount these horrible events of early childhood he seemed to become very uninvolved and unemotional. Actually, he was *recalling* the way he was betrayed but was not bringing into treatment his fear, anger, and fury over being so terribly abused and cruelly injured by both parents. It would seem that bringing this kind of material to the surface in therapy was a triumph, but this was not to be the case. Yes, he recalled the early childhood events, but emotionally he repeated the betrayal in the treatment situation.

Shortly after this material became a conscious memory, he began to feel that something was "missing" in his analysis. Then, for no apparent reason, he refused to lie down on the couch and totally resisted and completely dismissed any interpretations I made; nothing I said had any meaning for him. Something, he felt, was lacking in my treatment but he would not tell me what it was. I was being killed off. Then, after a month of his feeling "disappointed" with his therapy, he left me, saying he was going to find another therapist. It was clear that he wanted nothing to do with me (or with his transferential feelings).

Walt's leaving was probably a repetition of his feeling left alone and deserted, and was based on his reaction to the father's abandoning him in his childhood. The father betrayed him as he left him to his mother's cruelty and did not intercede and defend him against this maternal demon. As he gained some access to the feelings of the early traumatic material he probably expected (on some unconscious level) to be betrayed again by his therapist whom he had unconsciously made into a symbolic father. Unfortunately, he could not or would not let himself gain a true knowledge of what had really happened in his childhood, and so he betrayed himself and his analysis by leaving treatment.

In a self-defeating way Walt stayed loyal to his terrible, deceitful mother because he left therapy under her emotional influence, feeling distrustful and disappointed with a therapist who cared for him and his welfare.

DR. X

Doctor X is a therapist who can best be described as a very self-centered and narcissistic person. In a therapy session, when given the slightest cue, he will inappropriately intrude his own life experiences into the patient's treatment hour. In a deep and well-practiced baritone voice, he readily talks about his writing or his book. Of course, Dr. X can easily come out with his political opinions and intellectual ideas on any subject where he thinks he can show off his brilliance. He "works best" with those patients who, by the very nature of their conflicts, tend to be passive, submissive, and worshipful to those in authority.

In his true narcissistic fashion, he showers his own expansive self-esteem on those people who seek his professional help. He always feels that he is "the greatest" and projects this identification onto his patients and gives them the idea that they also are "the greatest." Then a kind of contract or ritual is formed as Dr. X repeatedly tells his patients that they are wonderful and he "loves" them. Eventually these patients, in return, feel compelled to tell him back that he is terrific and they love him. Unfortunately, there are submissive and dependent types of people who enjoy this kind of "therapy." These treatment victims may like to engage in this constant form of mutual flattery–and "enjoy" the sessions–but they will never get better, grow emotionally, or gain any insight into their problem. Such patients are betrayed by the narcissism of the analyst and are often drugged by "love and support" and never learn to be independent and insightful. Maturation does not become an issue since they receive so much "love." Psychotherapy is not a procedure for mutual flattery.

This type of therapist uses "warmth and loving feelings" and well-polished opinions on all subjects to inhibit and destroy the process of therapy, and through this "caring manner" betrays the very profession he or she claims to practice. The treatment hour belongs to the patient and is not a stage for the practitioner's theatrical use or abuse. It is interesting to note that this kind of therapy defeats the treatment process by making sure that no real and appropriate emotional discovery is made in the treatment hour. Unfortunately, this kind of "therapy" is quite common.

Any major defect in the personality of the therapist which is brought into the treatment setting has the potential to defeat the process of therapy (Finell, 1985). The sincere and honest practitioner tends to be quiet, to listen, to maybe ask an important question, and lets the patient do the talking. If the therapist is to talk at all, it must be in the service of helping the patient gain some insight or awareness; other than that, the therapist really has nothing to say. The time belongs to the patient.

A good therapist always works to keep his or her own mental house in good order and must have the inner honesty and personal strength to seek out supervision or additional personal treatment if he or she does not understand a patient or experiences a personal problem that interferes with the work of therapy. Being a therapist is not an easy job, neither is being a patient. Both positions demand dedication and honesty in every way possible. In life and in psychotherapy there is no substitute for honesty.

RALPH

Ralph, who had made many gains in therapy, announced one day that he wanted to leave treatment because he felt very misunderstood in his sessions with me. He was very sincere as he told me he saw no reason for continuing analytic work. When I questioned him about the areas in which he felt he had been misunderstood, he could not provide me with a single answer. He did insist that he felt very hurt and misunderstood but could not remember an instance where I had treated him insensitively or badly or had misunderstood him.

In exploring these feelings further we finally learned that this "not being understood" was his general reaction to being cruelly abused as a child. After working on this problem for awhile it became clear that his mother had taught him that no one could really value him. So, he was torn between a feeling that I would betray him by not understanding him or that he would betray himself because he could not accept any caring or interest. Happily, this problem was worked through in his analysis and Ralph learned to trust himself, his therapist, and others more.

Every patient has had some encounter with being betrayed, and betrayal can take an endless number of forms. Both the therapist and the patient have to work on this important problem at one time or another in many forms and settings.

When one gives up the ritual of unconsciously looking for and expecting betrayal from the other person, one is then freer to find relationships with truly loving people who are interested in being helpful, caring, and loving.

AFTERTHOUGHT

Blind trust as a lifelong position is just as destructive as blind distrust. In both cases the reality principle is abandoned, judgment is suspended, and the sense of self-caring is lost. There are people in the world who live to betray others, and that is a fact. Therefore, a sense of awareness and a small degree of suspicion in approaching and dealing with all life situations is a good and valid strategy. The healthy ego protects itself in the outer and inner worlds. Trust and distrust must be based on *fact*. People with blind trust in everyone are constantly in the process of setting themselves up to be eventually injured. The con man, the deceiver, and the criminal love to find those very friendly and naively trusting people, persons they can charm, manipulate, and eventually hurt.

One of the best things that one can achieve is a knowledge of how to be self-protective. Self-protection, as an attitude, begins with the awareness that a percentage of people do not care about the welfare of the other party, no matter how sincere or loving they may sound. Indeed, they are out to use, deceive, and hurt anyone they come across. One needs to strive to develop an ability to make proper reality judgments about other people, actions, situations, and choices. Proper judgments are aided by an awareness of the fact that people are not always what they seem, sound, or claim to be. Christ was aware of this fact when he told his disciples, "One of you will betray me."

If we work on structuring a moral and loving life situation and can treasure those who genuinely value us and our welfare, it is hard to be betrayed. You are whom you trust.

Mental disorders often involve the use of ego mechanisms where the world is distorted to issues of black and white (splitting), or issues of punishment and reward (borderline phenomenon), or idealization and devaluation (narcissistic condition), or masochism and sadism (submission and domination). In splitting, in the issue of punishment, or in the need for devaluation and domination, one is primed to hurt the other. In submission, in feeling rewarded, and in idealization one is placed in a position to be hurt by the other. Victimization begins with idealization, submission, and the naive expectation of a reward. For both patient and therapist, the issues of deception and betrayal have got to become a focus of treatment since so much of human interaction leads to some aspect of hurt and betrayal. The ability to avoid contact with abusive people and negative situations is a great ego strength and should be a treatment goal for every patient.

REFERENCES

Finell, J.S. (1985). Narcissistic problems in analysts. *International Journal of Psycho-Analysis, 66,* 433-439.
Klein, M. (1977). *Love, guilt and reparation.* New York: Dell.
    Shengold, L. (1985). *Soul murder.* New Haven: Yale University Press.
Winnicott, D.W. (1965). *The maturational processes and the facilitating environment.* New York: International Universities Press.

Voices of Betrayal

Janet Vice

SUMMARY. Part of the complexity of determining a given instance of betrayal lies in determining whether its occurrence results from an individual or a social moral failure. It may also be represented by a contradictory set of behaviors, depending upon the moral framework within which it is defined. Two competing indictments of psychiatric practice, those of Thomas Szasz and Peter Sedgwick, agree that psychiatry is guilty of patient betrayal. They also agree that the nature of that betrayal is psychiatry's violation of the personhood of its patients. But their definitions of personhood–Szasz's based on autonomy and Sedgwick's based on community membership–lead to radically different recommendations for psychiatric reform. The work of Carol Gilligan and her description of two competing moral "voices," each based on one part of the paradox of human experience, provides a moral framework within which Szasz's and Sedgwick's critiques emerge as exemplars of each "voice." Their apparent irreconcilability points to both the paradoxical nature of psychiatric practice and its necessary reliance upon moral reasoning.

Betrayal is a moral term and, like other moral terms, finds its conceptual home within relationships between individuals. It is commonly understood as a phenomenon internal to an existing relationship whose terms are moral in nature. This understanding depends upon the presupposition that the relationship itself is essentially moral. Thus betrayal, in violating the fiduciary foundation of the relationship, effectively destroys or seriously damages it.

But betrayal need not only occur *within* a given relationship. All relationships are social and political in nature, for their possibility,

Janet Vice, PhD, is Assistant Professor of Philosophy at California State University, Bakersfield and a Fellow of the Kegley Institute of Ethics. Mailing address: California State University, Bakersfield, Department of Philosophy and Religious Studies, 9001 Stockdale Highway, Bakersfield, CA 93311-1099.

as well as their range of structural options, is determined at the macro level of society. This means that one possible agenda for ethical social criticism is the examination of the moral foundations of certain social roles and the relationships which supervene on those roles. From this perspective, it is conceivable that betrayal appear independently of the behavior of individuals, yet as an integral part of their relationship, as a necessary element of the roles which make the relationship possible. The moral inference of such social criticism is that to participate in such a relationship on any basis is to be betrayed, irrespective of individual behavior.

Part of the complexity of determining a given instance of betrayal, therefore, lies in determining whether its occurrence results from an individual or a social moral failure. But there is a second complexity: the fact that individual moral judgments are made relative to an overarching moral framework or world view. This world view usually depends upon an ultimate principle which determines and structures moral action and, in so doing, defines the nature of moral failure as well. Betrayal, which is a form of moral failure, may therefore be represented by a widely disparate, even contradictory, set of behaviors, depending upon the moral framework which defines it.

Because the psychiatric doctor/patient relationship is fiduciary in nature, because it encompasses inequality of power and is initiated in patient vulnerability, the possibility of betrayal is unavoidable. The moral question, however, concerns the locus and nature of such betrayal, should it occur. Is it a moral failure of the doctor/therapist qua individual moral agent? Or are the roles of psychiatric therapist/patient so defined that betrayal is an unavoidable part of their relationship? Is that relationship, in fact, an example of "socialized" betrayal?

This is precisely the claim of two of contemporary psychiatry's most articulate and cogent critics, Thomas Szasz and Peter Sedgwick. Szasz is an American psychoanalyst and psychiatrist whose lengthy publishing career attacks psychiatric theory and practice from a liberal individualist perspective; the late Peter Sedgwick was a British psychologist whose major work, *Psycho Politics* (1982), outlines a powerful socialist critique of psychiatry. As psychiatry's critics they are polar opposites in their indictments and recommendations for psychiatric reform. Szasz's critique of psychiatry focuses on society's obligation (and failure) to respect the rights and freedom of psychiatric patients. Sedgwick is concerned with society's obligation (and failure) to provide living arrangements and medical services of a caliber which preserve and enhance personal dignity rather than sacrificing it. Yet both agree that the fundamental wrong which society must redress is that particular form of betrayal which is instantiated in the contemporary psychiatric doctor/patient relationship: psychiatry's (specifically institutional psychiatry's) violation of the personhood of its patients. Both argue that the price of becoming a psychiatric patient in our society is the loss of one's moral and communal status as a person.

For both Szasz and Sedgwick, betrayal means violation of the patient's personhood. But this shared claim, given the disparities of their definitions of personhood, ends in descriptions of betrayal which are polar opposites. In this study I shall compare and contrast Szasz's and Sedgwick's theories of personhood and the understanding of betrayal which each mandates. Using the work of Carol Gilligan and her gender-related "voices" of moral reasoning, I shall then outline a moral framework within which Szasz's and Sedgwick's apparently mutually exclusive arguments actually represent separate moral "voices," neither of which is complete without the other. I shall conclude that the challenge of reconciling Szasz's and Sedgwick's theories of psychiatric betrayal is the identical challenge which faces psychiatry in defining its own moral agenda.

SZASZ AND PERSONS

If personhood has an essence, then Szasz (1976) would identify that essence as autonomy. His work portrays humans as creative beings who must design their own lives free from the help or interference of others, much as a sculptor creates a figure from stone (p. 83). Autonomy is therefore not merely a normative ideal, but both a fact about the human condition and a sine qua non for human fulfillment. It is both a description of and a requirement for the essentially private act of self-creation.

Three claims follow from the centrality of autonomy. One is that it is possible to view the individual in abstraction from all others, that the self has in some sense a reality, an existence separate from any communal existence. In fact, the heart of its existence is private. The primacy of autonomy implies that logically, if not temporally, a person exists in and by oneself before existing in relationship to others.

The second claim is that this essentially solitary identity presupposes a certain degree of self-sufficiency. If the task of self-creation is by its very nature private, that can only be because the participation of others is not necessary to the process; if anything, it constitutes an impediment. This is not to claim that individuals have no genuine need for each other at any level. But if autonomy is central to personhood, then at the heart of selfhood lies a process which requires no other person's contribution. In fact, the interference of others in this process is sufficient to invalidate or to destroy it.

The third claim which follows from the primacy of autonomy concerns the importance of voluntary choice. The personal self-sufficiency which is expressed in self-creation is the direct result of free choice. One no longer has autonomy when one loses freedom of choice. Since autonomy is the center of personhood, an individual without choices is no longer a person.

Although autonomy is a fact about the human condition, it is not an irrevocable fact. When Szasz describes the human condition as essentially autonomous, he is speaking atheistically. Humans are free of a divinely ordered telos to which their selfhood must conform and by which their selfhood is somehow preordained. In this sense each person is a genuine creator of his or her own self.

Between humans, however, the possession of autonomy is a more precarious matter. Both it and the personhood for which it is the prerequisite may be betrayed or surrendered. The loss of human autonomy is always an evil: it can only be evil for individuals to choose or to be forced to become non-persons. But persons can surrender their personhood only to another person or persons; similarly, their personhood can be betrayed only by another person. The implication is that loss of autonomy–which, in Szasz's work, is the moral equivalent of original sin–is a continuous hazard attending interpersonal relationships.

Autonomy can also be sabotaged by the body. Loss of consciousness, paralysis, or brain disorders can render behavior non-voluntary or preclude the execution of personal choice. In such cases there is no moral stigma accompanying non-autonomous behavior. There is, however, a physical lesion whose presence in the body can be located, even when the chain of effects it initiates is imperfectly understood or incompletely known. When there is no demonstrable physical cause for behaviors which appear to be non-autonomous (particularly when, over a period of time, no lesion appears), one must assume, as part of one's moral duty to respect personhood, that the deviant individual's behavior is voluntary.

The primacy of autonomy determines Szasz's (1970) understanding of mental illness by providing a foundational truth about human nature in light of which the symptoms and behaviors characteristic of psychiatric diagnoses must be interpreted. That truth, simply stated, is that persons are beings who make free choices, and that humans retain their personhood so long as others do not forcibly interfere with them (p. 47). When deviant behavior (without an ascertainable organic cause) is interpreted in light of this truth, it emerges as voluntary. People with psychiatric symptoms behave the way they do because they choose to. The moral status of those choices may be dubious, but so long as they do not interfere with the autonomy of others, the individual's right to make them cannot be disputed.

Mental illness, therefore, cannot be interpreted as a genuine phenomenon on Szasz's autonomy model of personhood. In denying the central tenet of autonomy, the idea of mental illness reveals itself as fraudulent, a concept which denies the deviant individual's responsibility for his or her own behavior. It does so, moreover, without the credentials of an organic lesion (which, while it would destroy the condition's identity as "mental" illness, would at least justify the claim to non-responsibility). At best, then, mental illness is a misclassification. At worst, it is the means by which psychiatrists can betray the personhood of those under their care.

Szasz's model of personhood has significant implications not only for the status of mental illness but also for the reform of psychiatry, which means the reform of society's response to its deviant members. Szasz advocates reform of that response by accepting deviancy as a personal choice rather than invariably identifying it with inability to choose. To accept such behavior as voluntary is also to hold deviant persons responsible for their behavior. As long as that behavior poses no threat to another person's autonomy, deviants should be left alone to pursue it in peace. Should they prove dangerous to others (not, it is worth noting, to themselves) they have earned the response society keeps for lawbreakers. Such persons are not "sick"; they are criminals, and society is justified in treating them as such.

If this basic social reform were to be implemented, psychiatry would by no means disappear. Many persons, troubled by the difficulty of human existence (a difficulty which Szasz (1977) himself believes is of tragic proportions), develop problems in living which can be resolved only with the assistance of a trained professional (p. 28). But Szasz's view of personhood has two immensely important implications for society's understanding of and response to such problems. One is that all problems in living which qualify for psychiatric help turn out to be forms of impaired or inadequate autonomy. Therefore, the solution to problems for which psychiatric help is appropriate will always center around the development of greater autonomy. This is an educative rather than a curative process. It follows that psychiatry, properly understood, is a kind of educational activity. As such, it requires practitioners who themselves are highly autonomous so that they may be capable of teaching others how to develop autonomy. Psychiatry thus becomes a helping profession with the sole justification of assisting persons to develop their freedom and self-sufficiency.

This leads to the second implication: that all psychiatric services must be voluntarily sought. Entrance into therapy must be the result of an autonomous decision by the patient (one has the impression that part of Szasz's psychiatric reform would be dropping this term entirely from the psychiatric vocabulary). This means that the only justifiable form of psychiatry is "contract psychiatry": a therapeutic relationship based on mutual agreement by psychiatrist and client, and structured by their negotiation of its goals and limits.

Szasz sees the principle of contract as the cardinal antidote for the threats to autonomy inherent in the doctor/patient relationship. Contracts help to equalize the power imbalance between doctor and patient, so that the two may interact as equals. Equality makes reciprocity possible which, for Szasz, is the basis of justice, the primary social virtue. Szasz (1977) points out that contracts always favor the weaker members of a pair. Since the strong have the option of gaining their desires through force, they do not require the contract in order to obtain them, whereas the weak couldn't protect their interests without the assistance afforded by the contract (p. 120).

Contract psychiatry is described by Szasz (1965) in *The Ethics of Psychoanalysis*. An alternate name for contract psychiatry is autonomous psychotherapy, whose purpose is "the preservation and expansion of the client's autonomy" (p. 7). Such therapy is based not on fulfilling the client's needs but on fulfilling the terms of a contract agreed to by both therapist and client at the outset of the relationship. Autonomous psychotherapy promises not a cure of an illness but an education enabling the client to grow more autonomous than he has been.

The way the psychoanalyst educates the client is set out in the section entitled "The Method of Autonomous Psychotherapy," and can be summed up in a phrase: treat the client as one who is already autonomous. Szasz repeatedly cautions the psychoanalyst not to allow the patient to draw him or her into private relationships, not to contact relatives or employers on the patient's behalf, not to be used as a spokesperson or attorney for the patient.

The underlying assumption of this type of therapeutic program is that autonomy is a skill, like learning to speak a language or learning to type. One learns it by doing it, in the company of a qualified teacher, of course. One needs the teacher to point out errors and demonstrate new lessons (in other words, the teacher's value is instrumental), but the development of autonomy is essentially a private stance adopted by the client. It is not the relationship between teacher and client which transforms the client; if anything, it is the teacher's gentle insistence on preserving the limits of the relationship which is ultimately most beneficial.

To base the therapeutic relationship on autonomy is to make relatedness secondary to individuality in logical order and axiological priority. Autonomous individuals are in some essential sense separate from one another; hence, the highest priority for morality is the preservation of that separateness. It follows that, if individuals are separate, their ends are likewise separate, often competing. Therefore, relationships are justified by their instrumental nature. They allow individuals to pursue private ends which they could not attain in isolation.

Since ends vary and may clash, it follows that an underlying tension characterizes relationships with others. The more we need others, the more vulnerable we become to their manipulation or neglect, and the more of a burden we place upon them for our well-being. This view of human relatedness is essentially preventive: it attempts to minimize the ubiquitous dangers inherent in interdependence by emphasizing a fundamental separateness and relegating relatedness to a subsidiary role, a role which is both freely chosen and carefully kept within the individual's own control.

The particular threat posed by mental illness or, as Szasz prefers to call it, problems in living, is the threat of impaired autonomy. To rectify this threat, Szasz recommends a therapeutic relationship which itself is limited and controlled by the strictures of the contract. The patient freely decides what he or she wishes to get out of therapy, negotiates those wishes with the therapist, and commits to them formally. This mapping of the bounds of the relationship protects both therapist and client from an enmeshment which could threaten the autonomy of either or both.

PERSONS AND SEDGWICK

At the opposite pole from Szasz, Sedgwick identifies the criterion of personhood as community membership. The community provides a framework for action, a spectrum of possibilities for identity and achievement. Human activity is essentially collective in nature. This is partly because activities have a history and a tradition within which individual contributions become moments in an ongoing process. Sedgwick (1982) claims that serious work in the arts, for example, is always a collective achievement–a surprising statement in a culture in which creativity in the arts has always been considered a hallmark of individuality (p. 10).

A second reason that Sedgwick calls human activity essentially collective is that personal relationships are inevitably structured and influenced by the social, economic, and sexual roles of the participants. Frequently such roles determine whether a personal relationship is even a possibility. When it is, they outline its limitations and determine its internal governing rules. Roles belong to the community's macrostructure, and they have a history of their own which is part of the community's history. For this reason Sedgwick criticizes Erving Goffman for attempting to study one-on-one encounters within the asylum as if they were self-explanatory givens rather than products of a larger social/political context (p. 65). Any attempt to understand that context must include awareness of its history as well as of its present structure. Thus Sedgwick sees the interaction of two persons as an outcome of their connections to the institution of which they are a part, the culture in which that institution exists, and the past. No one is an island, for it is impossible to say who any particular person is without making reference, both tacitly and explicitly, to other people.

Three significant implications follow from this view of personhood. The first is that the notion of an "individual" as an entity whose identity exists apart from all others is little more than an intellectual abstraction. Like all abstractions, it is a distortion of reality—in this case, the reality of persons. This means that any social theory which is based on the idea of the individual in abstracto and which also seeks to modify actual human practices will be at best ineffectual, since it clashes with the nature of lived human experience. At worst it fosters betrayal, since it encourages people to act against their own natures.

In the second place, since all personal relationships occur within a community whose structure and values determine their nature and define their possibilities, it follows that personal relationships are in an important sense dependent upon the macrostructure of society. Whether a marriage, for example, is a "May/December romance," a case of "miscegenation," a "good match," "morganatic," or "invalid" is a judgment made not by the couple themselves but by the legal, social, economic, and axiological standards of the place and time in which they live. For Sedgwick, the most private relationships cannot be defined or understood without reference to the public.

Finally, if being a person means being a community member, it follows that no single individual is self-sufficient or self-determining. Self-sufficiency is a concept which is deceptive because it suppresses or ignores each person's essential dependence on the other members of the group. It also ignores their dependence on him or her. Even worse, it fails to take account of the individual's need of their dependence, insofar as being needed, being counted on, is an essential part of membership. Self-determination is as much an abstraction as "pure" individuality, since it suppresses the social context of tradition, ethical norms, and personal and professional roles out of which the individual chooses. The modern notion of self-determination, seen through the eyes of Sedgwick's theory, is comparable to attendance at a banquet. The menu has been selected by others, the food purchased by others, the work of cooking done by others, while the guests fatuously attribute autonomy to the decision of which of two main courses and three desserts they prefer. For Sedgwick, it is not the act of choice which is primary; it is rather the participation in the social context which makes choosing possible.

Sedgwick's view of personhood does not require, as does Szasz's, any denial of the reality of mental illness. All illnesses have a social component. They alter behavior and impair or threaten to impair one's functioning as a group member. In so doing, they change the role of the stricken person, whose plight initiates a call for intervention and explanation. Implicit in the demand for explanation is the community's recognition that any of its other members could be similarly stricken. The illness of any one person poses an implicit threat to the well-being of the group, a threat of a magnitude in direct proportion to the group's inability to identify and treat the condition.

Sedgwick's view advocates a change in the way physical illness is perceived. Currently medicine not only concentrates on the bodily aspect of illness but attempts to make that aspect the Aristotelian essence of the illness, relegating the psychological, social, and axiological components of the condition to the status of accidental properties. Yet, says Sedgwick, it is these components just as much as it is bodily alterations which cause a condition to be properly called an illness; indeed, the identification of a change in body structure as pathological is itself a value judgment, since the same change could also result from aging or normal fatigue after a stressful day. Moreover, there would be no reason to identify any condition as an illness were it not for the fact that human life and human flourishing are values of transcultural and transhistorical supremacy.

If Sedgwick's criterion of personhood has any major implications for the understanding of mental illness, it is to reveal the essential continuity it shares with physical illness, a continuity based on a shared nature. Sedgwick's view of all illness replaces the emphasis on the body with an emphasis on the social conditions of illness and on the kind of social response illness elicits (as well as on the values prompting that response). The community reveals its values through its response to the threat posed by illness. His conclusion is therefore that illness is a social phenomenon.

While Sedgwick's view of personhood can comfortably acknowledge the reality of mental illness, it requires a comprehensive change in the community's response to the mentally ill. That response has been channeled primarily through institutional psychiatry. For many people (especially those suffering from the major mental illnesses) the mental hospital has become family, career, and community. The hospital is not a genuine community, though. It is an accommodation for those who cannot make it in a real community. When the hospital becomes a home, it shelters those former community members who no longer belong. But if being a person means being a member of the community, then the community is the locus of personhood. The inescapable conclusion is that the chronic hospital patient, in being excluded from the community, has been pronounced and treated as a non-person. The institutional patient and the betrayed patient are thus identical.

The logic of this argument has much in common with that of the ancient Hebrew and Homeric cultures, for whom ostracism was tantamount to non-existence, a living death. One is a person only within the community. When one has been ejected from the group, it is impossible to define one's status, for all personal identity is defined within the framework of group membership. While some might argue that the term "mental patient" signifies a role and, therefore, a continuing membership, Sedgwick would disagree. Mental patients no more participate in the ordinary life of a community than do its prisoners or political exiles. Chronic hospitalization is life outside the community. As such, it is not a life suitable for persons.

Much of the perennial exclusion of the mentally ill is based on a misunderstanding of mental illness, says Sedgwick. To put it colloquially, most crazy people are not crazy all of the time. Most of them are capable of limited–sometimes surprisingly broad–participation in community life (if not immediately, then frequently over time). Many mentally ill persons are capable not only of participation in community affairs but also of genuine contributions to home and family. Although such contributions may be limited or intermittent, it is wrong to rule out their possibility a priori, especially when so much depends on a place in the community.

To say that many of the mentally ill want and need to function within the community is not to say that they are or can become self-supporting. It is therefore an essential part of Sedgwick's agenda that the state assume financial responsibility for these impaired citizens. It is also the state's responsibility to act as guardian–that is, to design structures of community life within which the mentally ill may participate as they are able, to "place" patients in settings which are appropriate to their needs, and to supervise the care of those who require temporary or permanent hospitalization. Many of these tasks can be organized and executed through the agency of institutional psychiatry. Institutional psychiatry still has a place as a social agent, but its custodial role should be secondary and peripheral. Its major focus should be the placement and monitoring of outpatients. By placing the mentally ill under the financial guardianship of the state, individual households can be relieved of much of the economic burden of their care, while the community as a whole affirms its responsibility for them as members.

Sedgwick's view of personhood leads to the conclusion that treating the mentally ill as persons necessitates a certain form of social/political/economic organization within which it is possible to make the proper response to these disabled community members. Transforming the institution of psychiatry thus requires transforming society itself. Collective change is for Sedgwick a prerequisite for significant improvement in the lives of individual community members.

In spite of polar oppositions on the nature of personhood and the function of psychiatry, Sedgwick and Szasz agree that those who are diagnosed mentally ill are and remain persons. Society's response to them must, therefore, consist of provisions suitable to the needs of persons. For Szasz, this means a recognition of the autonomy of the mentally ill. For Sedgwick, it means reaffirming their community membership and providing opportunities for them to live in the community.

Both Szasz and Sedgwick also share the same basic reason for their attacks on psychiatric theory and practice-that it betrays the mentally ill by treating them as non-persons. In fact, Szasz maintains that the term *mentally ill* is applied to a person for the express purpose of gaining legal and social authorization to treat him or her as a non-person.

These fundamental similarities of purpose make the contrasts between Szasz and Sedgwick all the more striking. They may be summarized in the following way. For Szasz, personhood emerges from within the single individual. For Sedgwick, personhood emerges from membership within a community. For Szasz, the privacy of individual self-creation makes interaction with other selves possible. For Sedgwick, interaction with others is an inescapable precondition of individuality. Szasz believes that ethical action results from deliberate, free choice from at least two possible alternatives. Sedgwick believes that ethical action results from conforming to a social structure within which "right" action is also a social norm.

These contrasts lead to contrasting views of mental illness and psychiatry. Szasz views deviant behavior as voluntarily chosen; he therefore denies that mental illness exists. Psychiatry's only purpose is to teach persons how to increase their autonomy. Its services should be restricted to those who voluntarily seek them. Sedgwick believes that deviant behavior is just as much outside individual control as is a fever or an infection. It is an involuntary inability to behave in accordance with the norms governing community membership. Psychiatry's role is to act with the community to create roles through which those with impaired social abilities can nevertheless enjoy the benefits of membership and participation. Psychiatry's purpose is not to supervise the ostracism of the mentally ill; it is to support the community in organizing their re-entry. The role of choice is paramount, but it is the choice of the community to make a place for its disabled members, not the choice of the disabled, which counts.

Szasz and Sedgwick appear to be exemplars of a moral stalemate. Each defines personhood in such a way that its betrayal appears to exclude the moral indictment posited by the other. Since both are critics of psychiatry, their divergence reveals a deep tension running through the psychiatric enterprise as a whole. I shall argue that this tension is inevitable, given the fundamental tension within human personhood, and that it arises from two radically different understandings of the moral life, each grounded in a disparate yet fundamental component of human experience.

SEPARATE YET RELATED

An episode from the science fiction television series *Star Trek* has the crew of the Enterprise responsible for transporting the Ambassador Kalos back to his native planet. Kalos belongs to a race of highly evolved beings whose superior mental energy is unimpeded by the weight of a body. Human beings cannot look directly at Kalos–who resembles a cloud of sparkling lights–without losing their sanity. He is therefore confined within a chest when humans are present.

A skeptical crew member snatches the chance to look at Kalos, goes insane, and seizes control of the Enterprise, taking it beyond a cosmic barrier never before crossed by humans. None of the crew has the navigational sophistication to pilot the ship out of this unknown territory. Kalos has the necessary skills; in order to gain access to his knowledge, Science Officer Spock performs the Vulcan mind-link, through which both Kalos's and Spock's minds inhabit Spock's body. Spock, guided by Kalos, safely returns the Enterprise to its former location.

In a brief, poignant sequence before the dissolving of the mind-link, Kalos, using Spock's voice, savors the new experience of embodiment. He expresses his curiosity and delight at the compactness of the human body and the pleasures of sense perception. Then a troubled expression comes over Spock's face. Kalos says, with wonder and compassion blended in his voice, "You are so alone!"

Kalos experiences embodiment as a separation from others, a boundary forbidding closer approach. His response is one of compassion and surprise at the existential loneliness of the human condition. The separateness which arouses his compassion is that same metaphysical foundation upon which the moral values of justice, reciprocity, autonomy, and universality of moral principles are laid.

What Kalos does not realize is that the body is more than a form of solitary confinement. Human beings are not merely separate selves or distinct bodies. They are persons, which means that they are characterized by their interactions as well as by their separateness. The body is not only a boundary denoting individuality; it is also a token denoting membership in the human community. It is a symbol of personhood, a sign that here is one who belongs, one of us. Kalos cannot truly understand being human until he becomes aware of the relationship (and, at times, the tension) between separateness and belonging.

Carol Gilligan's (1982) *In A Different Voice* postulates that these two principles of human existence, separateness and relatedness, give rise to two different views of the nature and purpose of the moral life. Gilligan refers to these views as "voices," and explains that they embody differences in emphasis which are gender-related, although not gender-specific.

The principle of human separateness is the fountainhead of the moral principles of justice, equality, autonomy, and reciprocity. When separateness is selected as the primary fact of human existence, its preservation and protection become the primary goals of the moral agenda. Thus separation gives rise to what Gilligan calls a "morality of fairness" (p. 19). Such a morality is formal in its structure, appealing to universalizable principles and rules of conduct.

It is also abstract, for the very process of moral decision making requires, as its prerequisite, the abstraction of the individual and his or her context as salient moral data.

Emphasis on separation and consequent allegiance to a morality of fairness are typical of masculine thinking, says Gilligan, because they reflect the masculine developmental process of separation from the mother. Because the male child is of the opposite sex from his primary caregiver, he learns that the development of personal identity is primarily a process of individuation. Thus men's experience teaches them that relatedness is secondary to and contingent upon individuation.

For women the reverse is true. Because the girl child's primary caregiver is apt to share her sex, her experience of identity is embedded in relationships, for she identifies with rather than separates from the mother. The world of feminine experience is a world in which individuality is secondary to and dependent upon relatedness.

A focus upon relatedness leads to a morality of responsibility and care, since duty is defined contextually and relative to specific relationships under consideration. There is thus no such moral entity as an abstract, universalizable moral judgment; moral judgments are required as responses (hence the name "morality of responsibility") to actual lived situations affecting or potentially affecting given relationships. Indeed, such judgments represent a way of specifying what, at this time and place, the relationship requires of the moral agent. As such, they provide a means of defining the relationship.

Men and women use both elements of reasoning in arriving at moral judgments, says Gilligan. Yet there is a marked tendency for one element to dominate moral reasoning in each sex. For men, it is the morality of fairness; for women, the morality of responsibility and care tends to be supreme.

Because these moral voices represent values which are themselves in tension with each other in human experience, each voice tends to be critical of the reasoning and judgments reached by the other. A morality of fairness is often accused of indifferentism and lack of concern for individuals, whereas a morality of responsibility can appear too diffuse and context-bound when judged from a perspective of universal principles (p. 22).

These criticisms, each of which is valid, point toward a deeper truth about morality: that each voice of moral reasoning, presenting as it does an ultimate principle based on only half of the paradox of human experience, is not so much an inaccurate explication of the moral life as it is an incomplete one. As Gilligan puts it, " . . . we know ourselves as separate only insofar as we live in connection with others, and . . . we experience relationship only insofar as we differentiate other from self" (p. 63).

Gilligan's model of competing moral voices provides a framework within which to explain the apparently irreconcilable critiques of Szasz and Sedgwick. Szasz's indictment of psychiatry and its patient betrayal is clearly based on the morality of fairness, in which separation is the primary fact about human life, as well as the primary value to be defended. Since relationships are essentially of instrumental value to the self, the ideal context for social interaction is one in which all selves are treated as equals. Mental illness, with its claim that universal autonomy is an intellectual fiction, therefore is interpreted by Szasz as a tool of betrayal, of society's betrayal of those of its citizens unfortunate enough to become "patients." The institution of psychiatry is the tool used by society to accomplish as well as to rationalize betrayal, defined by Szasz as the violation of separateness.

Sedgwick is just as clearly indicting psychiatric theory and practice from the perspective of a morality of responsibility and care. Since personhood is a result of relatedness, and individual relationships are made possible by the community and its values, it is the community's responsibility to preserve the membership status of all within it, particularly those whose impairments make them vulnerable to the loss of their membership and, with it, the loss of their personhood. Society betrays psychiatric patients by isolating them from those forms of community interaction and membership which make personhood possible. Betrayal is thus defined as the violation of relatedness.

Is personhood the result of separateness or relatedness? Since each depends upon, even presupposes, the other, such a distinction creates a distorted view of persons. The intrinsic connection between separateness and relatedness becomes particularly clear when examining the effect of mental illness on personhood. As the capacity of the mentally ill to function as individuals becomes subordinated to the symptoms of their diseases, so, in direct proportion, does their ability to relate to others. The cost of impaired individuality is impaired relatedness, and vice versa.

Because Szasz and Sedgwick approach psychiatry from two different moral perspectives, their understanding of psychiatry's nature and purpose is at odds. The view of psychiatry resulting from the assumption that autonomy and its protection are paramount values appears to bear little relation to the view which results from the desire to restore and protect interrelatedness. Yet, if personhood requires both, then it makes sense that both are vulnerable to impairment, whether we term such impairment "mental illness" or "problems in living."

If this is so, then any moral mandate for psychiatry must specify its ability to deal with both kinds of threats to personhood. And which means of dealing with those threats is most therapeutic (and most morally justifiable) will necessarily depend upon the context within which they occur. There will be cases in which the outstanding symptom is loss of or failure to develop personal autonomy, others whose treatment requires immediate attention to an impairment of relatedness, and still others which will present both, alternatively or together. The two voices of morality, reflecting as they do the dual nature of human experience, make it impossible to specify, out of context, one single mandate to govern psychiatric practice. Psychiatry, like human life itself, must learn to live with its own paradoxes, its own contradictory tendencies, which means that psychiatric practice, if it is to avoid the betrayal of those whose pain justifies its existence as a therapeutic activity, cannot be practiced successfully without recourse to moral reasoning: ideally, a moral reasoning to which both voices can contribute and within which both voices can be heard.

REFERENCES

Gilligan, C. (1982). *In a different voice*. Cambridge, MA: Harvard University Press.

Sedgwick, P. (1982). *Psycho politics*. New York: Harper & Row.

Szasz, T. (1965). *The ethics of psychoanalysis*. New York: Basic Books.

Szasz, T. (1970). *Ideology and insanity*. Garden City, NY: Anchor Books.

Szasz, T. (1976). *Schizophrenia: the sacred symbol of psychiatry*. New York: Basic Books.

Szasz, T. (1977). *The theology of medicine*. Baton Rouge: Louisiana State University Press.

Szasz, T. (1987). *Insanity: the idea and its consequences*. New York: John Wiley and Sons.

Therapists' Personal Maturity and Therapeutic Success: How Strong Is the Link?

Kirk J. Schneider

SUMMARY. This article investigates the hypothesis that therapists' personal (psychological) maturity is a key factor in therapeutic effectiveness. Maturity is defined in terms of intra- and interpersonal openness, acceptance, and genuineness. Effectiveness is defined in terms of therapeutic process and outcome. The article reviews the literature pertinent to this topic from the standpoint of therapeutic theory and research. Although the results of this review indicate provisional support and far-reaching political and professional implications for the hypothesis, notable limitations in the data preclude a more definitive conclusion.

A leading contention of humanistic research in recent years (and one which other "schools" are beginning to endorse, e.g., see Lazarus, 1985; Orlinsky & Howard, 1978) is that the best therapists are "real," genuinely mature people. To put it another way, these researchers believe that the best therapists are not only facilitative (warm, accepting, etc.) with their clients, but also toward themselves and close others in their lives. Carl Rogers (1980), the foremost spokesperson for this view, summarizes:

Kirk J. Schneider, PhD, is a licensed psychologist and director of the Center for Existential Therapy in San Francisco, CA. He is the author of two books, *The Paradoxical Self* (Plenum, 1990) and *Horror and the Holy: Wisdom-teachings of the Monster Tale* (Open Court, in press). Currently, he is co-authoring a textbook in existential psychology (with Rollo May), and teaching at the California School of Professional Psychology, Berkeley/Alameda, CA. Mailing address: The Center for Existential Therapy, 2152 Union Street, San Francisco, CA 94123.

As I have considered . . . my own experience in the training of therapists, come to the somewhat uncomfortable conclusion that the more psychologically mature and integrated the therapist is, the more helpful is the relationship he or she provides. This puts a heavy emphasis on the therapist as a person. (p. 148)

The phrase "uncomfortable conclusion" in Roger's statement is a telling one. For in spite of the increased research on therapists' skills and attitudes (Beutler, Crago, & Arizmendi, 1986), and therapists as people (Burton, 1972; McConnaughy, 1987), curiously, little research has focused specifically on therapists' maturity (Beutler et al., 1986). One only has to witness the paltry number of relevant studies, for example, in major reviews (e.g., Beutler et al., 1986; Orlinsky & Howard, 1978; Parloff, Waskow, & Wolfe, 1978).

Although many reasons may account for this resistance-such as the complexity of the issue and the practical problems of conducting research–three in particular stand out. First, supportive results could lead to conflicts of interest for many traditional training programs. Their emphasis on the acquisition of skills and theory, as opposed to personal growth, might soon be viewed with a great deal of suspicion, if not outright disdain. Accordingly, traditional institutions might be forced to change many of their "sacred" and established practices. Second, evidence supporting the view that maturity is a key factor in therapists' success increases the likelihood that paraprofessional or relatively untrained helpers would proliferate–threatening to replace many professionals.

On the other hand, if the evidence weighs against maturity as a key factor in therapists' success, then humanistically oriented schools would receive a jolt. It may be, they would find, that factors such as warmth and genuineness are either irrelevant or technically controlled, and this would run counter to their central beliefs.

In a strongly worded statement, Oden (1974) elaborates on why so many researchers are reluctant to confront the above potential consequences:

When I ask myself the reason why [these issues are] so sensitive, the most apparent answer is that [they] appear to challenge the very foundations of the professionalization process in psychotherapy which understandably has vested interests against the line of inquiry we are pursuing. (p. 11)

On the pages to follow, I will pursue this line of inquiry against which–we can safely assume–there are vested interests. I will look at the literature pertinent to the hypothesis that therapists' personal maturity is a key factor in their effectiveness.

To redress the vagueness of past research on therapists' maturity (Beutler et al., 1986), I will now propose an operational definition for the term. This definition reflects the humanistic standpoint, and comprises the following three dimensions: (a) the therapist is *intrapersonally* mature. This means that the therapist has learned to deal effectively with problems in his or her life, and is comparatively open (capable of surveying what is within), accepting (capable of valuing, relating to, or understanding what is within), and genuine (capable of acknowledging, expressing, or actualizing what is within). (b) The therapist is *interpersonally* mature. Mature in this respect means that the therapist has learned to cope or help with the problems of others (especially close others), and is comparatively open, accepting, and genuine with them. (c) The therapist's maturity is seen as a *process* and not a state. This means that maturity rests on a continuum. One cannot be said to be mature in all places and at all times, or to have completely resolved one's problems. By contrast, maturity is viewed here as the sustained effort to deal constructively with problems, even if that effort entails temporary setbacks.

My operational definition for "effectiveness" concerns, broadly, the quality of the therapeutic relationship. Specifically, therapeutic effectiveness is defined in terms of *outcome* (post-therapy client change) and *process* (constructiveness of therapists' response).

The first part of this article will address theoretical literature linking therapists' maturity and effectiveness; the second part will consider the experimental research; and the third will attend to evidence from the research on paraprofessional help. Finally, I will discuss the limitations of the extant evidence, and suggest which conclusions we can draw at this point.

THEORETICAL LITERATURE

A number of theorists who are practicing therapists have specu-
lated about the relevance of therapists' maturity to therapy, and a
sample will be noted here. While all of the theoretical evidence (of
which I am aware) espouses a positive association between maturity
and effectiveness, its centrality varies and is sometimes misconstrued.

Despite many psychoanalysts' overriding concern with technique (Luborsky & Spence, 1978), they were perhaps the first to
focus on therapists' maturity. Freud (1912/1958), for example,
wrote that the psychoanalyst "should have undergone a psychoanalytic purification and have become aware of those complexes of his
own which would be apt to interfere with his grasp of what the
patient tells him" (p. 116).

In 1934, Jung (1964) addressed the issue more squarely. He
wrote that it was "largely immaterial what sort of techniques [the
therapist] uses, for the point is not technique . . . the personality and
attitude of the doctor are of supreme importance" (pp. 159-160).

The early psychoanalysts Sachs and Fromm-Reichman also
stressed the importance of therapists' maturity (see also Reik,
1948). Sachs (1947), for example, contended that "psychoanalysis
demands all of a man's humanity: it appeals constantly to the entire
person" (p. 162). Fromm-Reichman (1950) elaborated on the position that self-integration and personal maturity are the hallmarks of
the best therapists. She wrote:

> If it is true that the therapist must avoid reacting to patients'
> data in terms of his own life experience, this means that he
> must have enough sources of satisfaction and security in his
> non-professional life to forego the temptation of using his
> patients for the pursuit of his personal satisfaction and securi-
> ty. (p. 7)

Contemporary theorists such as Rogers, Bugental, and Jourard,
refined the views of their predecessors and developed more elabo-
rate theories of therapists' maturity. Rogers (1961), for example,
defined maturity in terms of his own personality theory. He asserted
that the best therapists are "fully-functioning" people. They are

more open to experience, live in the present, and trust their creative and intuitive perceptions. Bugental (1976) and Jourard (1976) emphasized the importance of authenticity or genuineness in the therapist. They contended that the best therapists are those who gained some mastery of their inner turmoil. Jourard (1976) intoned:

The great psychotherapists are exemplars at taming and transcending some aspect of the factical world that subjugates most of us . . . a therapist cannot himself lead a person to a freer . . . existence than he himself has attained. (pp. 39-40)

EXPERIMENTAL EVIDENCE

What follows is a survey of experimental evidence which compares therapists' maturity to their effectiveness. Although this survey is not exhaustive, it is based heavily on major reviews and is therefore representative, I believe, of the contemporary maturity/effectiveness literature. Three vantage points are used to assess this issue: personal therapy and effectiveness; experience level and effectiveness; and multimodal ratings of maturity and effectiveness. Each of these domains encompasses a variety of empirical and psychometric means of assessment. The criterion "effectiveness," it will be recalled, is defined in terms of outcome (post-therapy client change) and process (constructiveness of therapists' responses).

Personal Therapy and Effectiveness

Based on the theoretical literature, one would assume that therapists' personal therapy is a key factor in the fostering of their maturity and, in turn, effectiveness. A perusal of the empirical literature, however, suggests a much less clear picture (Beutler et al., 1986; Parloff et al., 1978).

Peebles (1980) and Buckley, Karasu, and Charles (1981), for example, found that good personal therapy has mutative effects. Most of the therapists in their samples who had undergone such treatment offered higher levels of warmth, empathy, and genuineness to their clients. Strupp (1955) and McNair, Lorr, Young, Roth, and Boyd (1964) also found that personal treatment for therapists associated with effective therapeutic process and outcome with clients.

On the other hand, Holt and Luborsky (1958); McNair, Lorr, and Callahan (1963); and Garfield and Bergin (1971) found no such beneficial effects from personal treatment. Garfield and Bergin (1971) even went so far as to report that some personal treatment associated with poor counseling, and that an extensive amount associated with even *worse* results. The fact that some therapists were in treatment at the time they were being studied, however, may have distorted these findings.

The research on personal therapy, in addition to being contradictory, is also plagued by methodological problems. Therapists' need for treatment and the success or failure of treatment are rarely reported in detail (Parloff et al., 1978). Without these data it is unclear whether therapists' effectiveness or ineffectiveness is due more to their intrinsic emotional state or to the quality of their treatment.

Overall then, the evidence concerning personal therapy is contradictory and methodologically flawed (Beutler et al, 1986). It remains for future research to provide a clearer consensus.

Experience and Effectiveness

Another factor that is often linked to therapists' maturity and effectiveness is their experience level (Beutler et al., 1986). It is logically assumed that such factors as therapists' age and their clinical and life experiences are associated with their maturity and expertise. Yet, as with the studies on personal therapy, this field too is pervaded by contradictory findings and methodological flaws, although there appears to be a recent reversal of this situation (Beutler et al., 1986; Hellman, Morrison, & Abramowitz, 1987). Several extensive reviews suffice to give a representative picture.

Luborsky, Chandler, Aurbach, Cohen, and Bachrach (1971) found that 8 out of 13 studies showed a significant positive correlation between therapists' age and clients' improvement. Bergin (1971) and Meltzoff and Kornreich (1970) also concluded that experience seemed to make a positive difference in process and outcome studies.

Aurbach and Johnson (1977), on the other hand, reported far less supportive evidence. They found that only 5 out of 12 studies favored the experienced therapists. Parloff et al. (1978) found that only 4 out of 13 studies supported the experienced therapist. Smith, Glass, and Miller (1980), likewise, found that the average effect-size estimates attributable to therapists' experience were negligible.

In the most extensive meta-analysis to date, Stein and Lambert (1984) found few general effects on experience and outcome. However, by statistically controlling certain variables and comparing others, they found that positive effects of experience were *most* likely to emerge when: (a) therapists' experience levels were distinct; (b) patients were difficult; (c) complex and intensive treatments were studied; and (d) the outcome variables were assessed early or included drop out rates (Beutler et al., 1986; Stein & Lambert, 1984). One possible explanation for these findings is that experienced therapists possess a greater degree of comfort, flexibility, and confidence than inexperienced therapists do in difficult clinical situations (Faber & Heifitz, 1981; Hellman et al., 1987).

The net effect of these and related studies prompted reviewers to acknowledge that although the research on experience and effectiveness is beset by contradictory findings and methodological flaws (e.g., a lack of homogeneity among clients who see more or less experienced therapists, a lack of clear agreement as to how to define "experience" and therapeutic effectiveness, Beutler et al. 1986; Parloff et al., 1978), the following can be said: Therapists' "experience exerts a complex effect that is most observable either on psychotherapy processes, early treatment gains, or dropout rates" (Beutler et al., 1986, p. 287; Stein & Lambert, 1984). Experienced therapists' level of comfort, flexibility, and confidence (factors closely related to intra- and interpersonal openness, acceptance, and genuineness), it may be added, appears to be the partial basis for this conclusion.

Multimodal Ratings of Maturity and Effectiveness

The use of multimodal ratings is yet another approach to assessing therapists' maturity and effectiveness. The ratings by peers, supervisors, and tests of psychological health are proposed to be strong indicators of therapists' personal and professional functioning (Parloff et al. 1978). Although the vast majority of these studies are supportive of the maturity/effectiveness link, a few are not, and I will note possible reasons for this contradiction as we proceed. Finally, it must be kept in mind that the following data are subject to substantial methodological limitations, which I will address in a later section.

Holt and Luborsky (1958) were, to my knowledge, the first investigators to extensively compare therapists' maturity and effectiveness. In a large-scale study of psychiatric trainees, the researchers found that the best possessed characteristics of the "good" person in general, as rated by peers, supervisors, and psychological tests. Specifically, Holt and Luborsky (1958) found that superior trainees possessed traits similar to our (aforementioned) definition of maturity. They were genuine, self-confident and secure, and had a high capacity for growth.

In a related study, Parloff (1956) looked at therapists' attitudes toward acquaintances (e.g., subordinates at a clinic) and toward a sample of outpatient neurotics. He found that the better therapists (as judged by colleagues and subordinates) were also better at establishing healthy social relationships. The traits which the judges found to characterize the better therapists were greater tolerance and respect for others, and self-confidence.

Ellsworth and Allen examined therapists' maturity and therapeutic process issues. Specifically, the investigators compared therapists' capacity for feeling verbalization both in and out of the therapy setting. Ellsworth (1963), for instance, compared the feeling verbalizations–affective as opposed to intellectualized statements–of therapists with their clients and with colleagues in case conferences. He found that there was a significant positive correlation between the amount of feeling verbalized by therapists in therapy and nontherapy settings. Allen (1967), correspondingly, compared therapists' openness to self and others using a similar rating of feeling verbalization. He also studied this dimension in counseling and noncounseling (case conference) settings and found a significant positive relationship. Significantly, Beutler et al. (1986), found that therapists' ability to handle and facilitate the expression of affect appears to be a "beneficial" (cross-disciplinary) therapeutic dimension (p. 294).

Using the ratings of independent judges and faculty supervisors, Combs and Soper (1963) found, with regard to the perceptual organization of the best counselor-trainees, the following: With respect to general perceptions, good counselors tend to (a) perceive from an internal rather than external frame of reference; and (b) in terms of people rather than things. With respect to other people, good counselors tend to (a) perceive them as able rather than unable; (b) friendly rather than unfriendly; (c) dependable rather than undependable; and (d) worthy rather than unworthy. With respect to themselves, good counselors tend to (a) identify with people rather than apart from them; (b) see themselves as enough rather than wanting; and (c) be self-revealing rather than self-concealing. Finally, with respect to values, good counselors tend to see themselves as (a) freeing rather controlling; (b) altruistic rather than narcissistic; and (c) involving themselves in larger rather than smaller contexts or meanings. Clearly, therapists' openness, acceptance, and genuineness are significant (if not the core) dimensions of these data.

The intra- and interpersonal maturity of therapists has also been examined from several other standpoints. These include the assessments of "expert" judges, clients, and psychological tests.

Fiedler (1950), for example, found in a pooling of expert opinion about the ideal therapist the following: Technique or theoretical background are relatively unimportant. What counts is that the therapist is able to "participate completely in the patient's communication," understand that patient's feelings, and convey his or her ability to share them (p. 353).

During the course of over two decades of research, the client-centered school has amassed a great deal of data which implies the importance of therapists' psychological maturity (Gurman & Razin, 1977; Truax & Carkhuff, 1967; Truax and Mitchell, 1971). Using the ratings of clinical judges and clients, these researchers have found modest to strong associations between therapists' empathy, warmth, and congruence (Parloff et al., 1978).

Clients' perceptions, in particular, have been the focus of growing attention by client-centered and other researchers. It appears that clients–as opposed to independent judges–make the most accurate predictions about their therapists' effectiveness (Gurman, 1977; Parloff et al., 1978). Interestingly, the qualities they cite as pivotal bear direct relation to therapists' openness, acceptance, and genuineness (Schneider, 1984). A study by Strupp, Fox, and Lessler (1969) serves to illustrate this point:

> The patients' preference was clear, they found a "human" therapist helpful.
> The composite image of the "good therapist" drawn by our respondents is thus that of a keenly attentive, interested, benign, and concerned listener–a friend who is warm and natural, is not averse to giving direct advice, who speaks one's language, makes sense, and rarely arouses intense anger. (p. 117)

Still other studies which have linked therapists' maturity to process and outcome have employed the evaluations of psychological tests.

In a study of self-actualization (as measured by the Personal Orientation Inventory) Foulds (1969) found that the dimension significantly related to therapists' genuineness, empathy, and warmth. Specifically, he found that such characteristics as "the ability to be open and disclosing of one's authentic being, . . . acceptance of oneself in spite of weaknesses, . . . and the ability to develop contactful intimate relationships" related to the therapists' in-role offerings of genuineness, empathy, and warmth (p. 90).

In a study of therapists' accurate empathy and empathic style of self-report, Fish (1970) found a positive correlation. His study suggested that the therapist's openness to his/her own feelings (as demonstrated in a self-report) associated with the therapist's openness and acceptance toward his/her clients. Bare (1967), similarly found that therapists who are more creative and express less need for social approval (as measured by a psychological test), also appear to be more empathic and helpful to clients.

Finally, Jackson and Thompson (1971), Burton (1972), and Gurman (1972) found that interpersonal fulfillment in therapists' outside lives is related to effective counseling. Specifically, Jackson and Thompson (1971) discovered that the best therapists have more positive attitudes toward themselves, most people, and most clients.

After studying the lives of 12 eminent therapists, Burton (1972) concluded that the personal capacity to cope with adversity had positive implications for professional performances. Similarly, Gurman (1972) found that effective therapists are generally more satisfied with their lives. "Most major reviews," conclude Beutler et al. (1986), favor "improvement in depression and defensiveness among patients whose therapists had the lowest levels of emotional disturbance" (p. 272).

At the same time that research has shown that certain "mature" qualities are related to therapists' effectiveness, another body of research (albeit smaller) has indicated that certain "immature" (or reverse) qualities are related to therapists' ineffectiveness. Bandura, Lipsher, and Miller (1960), for example, found that therapists who were rated as possessing anxiety conflicts and high needs for social approval also seem to be less effective with clients. Bergin (1966) provided a similar finding.

Several researchers have used the MMPI (Minnesota Multiphasic Personality Inventory) (e.g., Wogan, 1970; Garfield & Bergin, 1971; and Bergin & Jasper, 1969), and the TAT (Thematic Apperception Test) (e.g., Vandenbos & Karon, 1971), and found similar role/personality correlations. Wogan (1970), for example, found repressiveness to correlate negatively with therapists' effectiveness. Bergin and Jasper (1969) found high anxiety and depression to be negatively correlated with therapists' empathy; and Vandenbos and Karon (1971) showed that therapists' rated high on "pathogenesis" were less effective with schizophrenics after a 6 month period.

Despite the predominance of studies favorable to the maturity/effectiveness link, a few studies have indicated that there is no such association.

Using the ratings of supervisors, Streitfeld (1959), for example, found no clear correlation between therapists' expressed acceptance self and others and their effectiveness as counselors. Passons and Olsen (1969) found that therapists' openmindedness (as rated by the Rokeach Dogmatism Scale) is unrelated to empathic sensitivity with clients. Rowe and Winborn (1973), in a replication of the previously mentioned Foulds (1969) study, found that self-actualization (as measured by the POI) seems unrelated to therapists' offerings of genuineness, empathy, and warmth. Jackson and Thompson (1971), finally, found that both effective and ineffective therapists rated about the same on dimensions of cognitive flexibility and tolerance of ambiguity.

The above lack of support for the maturity/effectiveness link may well be illustrative of a problem which plagues all psychotherapy research: weak methodology due to poor construct validity and operational definitions (Orlinsky & Howard, 1978). For example, in the Jackson and Thompson study, it is questionable whether "cognitive flexibility" is equivalent to such earlier defined dimensions as "self and other acceptance" and "openness to feelings," which are more affective in tone. A similar problem may exist with respect to Passons and Olsen's "openmindedness," as rated by Rokeach's Dogmatism Scale, and effectiveness. It remains to be seen, moreover, as Rowe and Winborn's (1973) findings bear out, if a measure such as the POI truly reflects the concept of self-actualization. Until factors such as the above are clarified, the small number of contradictory findings presented here are not convincing. The overwhelming evidence in support of the maturity/effectiveness link, on the other hand (given its methodological weaknesses), must be regarded as more salient at this time.

PARAPROFESSIONAL STUDIES AND THERAPISTS' MATURITY

An alternative way to view the maturity/effectiveness issue is from the perspective of paraprofessional (or "lay" studies). If the formally untrained can be shown to be as mature and helpful as the professional, considerable light will have been shed on this article's chief concern–that is, the extent to which therapists' personal maturity affects their therapeutic success. Indeed, the evidence (given its limitations which will be noted later) is strikingly favorable to the maturity/effectiveness association.

The research on paraprofessional help derives from two general sources: anecdotal data and a growing body of empirical research. A representative sample of anecdotal data can be found in reports by such groups as Alcoholics Anonymous, Synanon, and former psychiatric patients turned counselors (Gibb, 1971). Although such groups have rarely participated in controlled studies (see Oden, 1974), they are thought to have positive therapeutic value (Gibb, 1971; Laing, 1969). One leading rationale for this conclusion is that participants have themselves achieved what they are trying to facilitate in others (Jourard, 1976). Stated more specifically, former alcoholics and psychiatric patients have learned to accept and deal with their own past "immaturity" which in turn gives them a "natural" empathy and capacity to deal with others' concerns.

Empirical research appears to confirm the anecdotal evidence, suggesting, in addition, that good helpers are both mature and do not require formal training.

Maslow (1954), for example, was a pioneer of research on the intimate relationships of persons with little or no formal therapy training. He found that among so-called self-actualizing people, most related to others in close, growth-promoting ways. Self-actualizers were helpful, genuine, open, and accepting *people,* Maslow reported.

Shapiro, Krauss, and Truax (1969) found that parents and close friends who were rated (by a relationship inventory) as congruent, warm, and empathic induced a variety of experimental subjects (e.g., undergraduates, police candidates, psychiatric patients) to disclose and relate more fully than did controls who lacked the aforementioned qualities.

Shapiro and Voog (1969) found, correspondingly, that undergraduate college students who offered high levels of genuineness, empathy, and warmth to their roommates appeared to promote those roommates' academic achievement better than controls who offered low levels. In a comparison of students' expectations of a counseling session with friends, Parham and Tinsley (1980) found equivalently supportive results. Specifically, their findings suggested that students highly valued accepting, confrontative, and trustworthy friends. Comparatively less emphasis was placed on the friend's being empathic, expert, or directive. In a study of disturbed adolescent boys, Goodman (1972) found that untrained "companions" of these boys discriminated on characteristics of maturity. In particular, he found that companions with high scores on openness, understanding, and warmth facilitated more psychological gains than those with lower scores.

Other studies have compared untrained helpers to trained or professional therapists, and have found correspondingly positive results. For example, Strupp and Hadley (1979) indicated from their investigation of professional therapists and nonexpert college professors, that the two groups did not differ significantly as counselors. Creaser and Carsello (1979), similarly, found that graduate students (some of whom had no formal training) were better able than professional therapists to relate to prospective students' concerns about becoming college students. The authors cited the graduate students' greater sensitivity to and identification with the prospective students' problems as the relevant facilitative factors.

After a review of 42 studies which compared paraprofessional and professional effectiveness, Lorian and Felner (1986) concluded:

1. Paraprofessionals are at least as effective as professionals.
2. Methodologically sophisticated studies favor paraprofessionals.
3. Levels of experience and training relate to paraprofessional effectiveness. (p. 763)

While these and similar findings by Durlak (1979) do not settle the maturity/effectiveness question, they do, by implication, highly favor the *likelihood* and *significance* of such an association.

LIMITATIONS OF THE DATA

Key limitations characterize the literature on therapists' personal maturity and effectiveness, and a representative sample will be presented here.

First, while it is clear that therapists' maturity is important, this review did not directly address the influence of other personal or social factors. These too may be important, and temper the significance of the aforementioned findings (Beutler et al., 1986). Moreover, the review did not directly address whether therapists' maturity is more or less important than therapists' technical skills. The rather persistent implication, however, especially in light of client-based and paraprofessional data, is that skills are of secondary importance (see also Gurman & Razin, 1977, p. xv; Strupp, 1972).

Second, the literature on personal therapy can be all but cast aside. It is far too equivocal at this point to relate in any meaningful way.

Third, there is the glaring problem of defining terms. Both maturity and effectiveness are controversial concepts and there seems to be vague agreement as to what they constitute (Gurman & Razin, 1977; Parloff et al., 1978). For example, do terms such as cognitive flexibility, tolerance, openness, acceptance and so on refer to the same or different constructs? What are the differences, if any, between clients' and "experts'" judgments of these terms? What does it mean to deal "constructively" with one's problems; does it mean that one is constantly trying to make things tidy or calm (perhaps denying feelings in the process), or does it signify periods of arduous confrontation (i.e., such as in the psychoanalytic sense of "regressing in the service of the ego")? Similarly, what is meant by "effective" therapy. Are clients and professionals perceiving different standards? Are subtle nuances in the therapeutic process being properly "teased out"? Researchers are not in clear agreement about these issues (Bergin & Lambert, 1978), and have often employed a variety of conflicting criteria (Parloff et al., 1978).

The research on maturity and effectiveness is also limited by a pervasive superficiality. One, there is a striking lack of data on the topic (Beutler et al., 1986). As mentioned earlier, there seems to be a collective resistance to examining the issue. Two, the research is indirect or partial. Areas such as the personal therapy and experience of the therapist account for only a small portion of the therapist's life. Similarly, therapists' interactions with supervisors, peers, and clients do not suffice to give us a representative picture of their lives. Therapists (as well as paraprofessionals) may respond differently when they are formally helping or consulting than when they are informally engaged. Even psychological tests do not fully tap therapists' level of maturity because while they reveal something about intrapersonal functioning, they have little to say about therapists' interpersonal experience and behavior. Given this data, then, we are limited in what we can infer about therapists' maturational *consistency,* and hence, Rogers' (1980) concept of the "therapist as a person."

The research on maturity and effectiveness, finally, is limited by the assessment devices employed. The use of rating scales, psychological tests, and audio/visual recordings to assess the personal qualities of therapists has all been criticized (Parloff et al., 1978). Audio and video recording, for example, has been criticized for its lack of sensitivity to subtle nuances of behavior. Tests and rating scales have been questioned in terms of their susceptibility to validity (especially construct validity) and reliability problems (Anastasi, 1976; Parloff et al., 1978).

DISCUSSION

This article investigated the hypothesis that therapists' personal maturity is a key factor in their effectiveness as professionals. Therapists' maturity was operationally defined in terms of intra- and interpersonal openness (capacity to survey what is presented), acceptance (capacity to value, relate to, or understand what is presented), and genuineness (capacity to acknowledge, express, or actualize what is presented). Maturity was also defined as a process, not a state. Therapists' effectiveness was operationally defined in terms of therapeutic process (constructiveness of therapists' responses) and outcome (post-therapy client change).

Five sections of the article focused on the hypothesis: theoretical literature, personal therapy and effectiveness, experience and effectiveness, multimodal ratings of therapists' maturity and effectiveness, and the paraprofessional literature and effectiveness.

Taken as a whole, I find the hypothesis substantively, although provisionally, confirmed. The preponderance of evidence reviewed suggests that therapists' personal maturity (as defined) is appreciably (if not predominantly) related to their professional success. This conclusion, however, is provisional. It is limited by a significant number of methodological flaws and contradictory findings.

Several implications arise from the data. First, many methodological and theoretical problems must be dealt with before firmer conclusions can be drawn. Second, there is a great deal more that can be learned about paraprofessional helping strategies. Increased research in this area is urgent, not only for its relevance to the question of therapists' personal maturity, but also for its relevance to the issue of helpers' education and experience. Third, if it is true that client factors (such as initial disposition, values) account for the "lion's share" of therapeutic change variance (Gurman, 1977), then more studies should concentrate on *clients'* perceptions to clarify the nature and importance of the maturity dimension (Schneider, 1984). Fourth, there are many interesting and potentially fruitful ways of approaching the topic of therapists' maturity. One such approach might entail a comparison of relationship inventories (or interviews) of both therapists' professional and nonprofessional contacts.

Despite its provisional nature, this review raises serious questions about the professional institution of psychotherapy. Not only do the findings (especially paraprofessional and client-based) uphold the importance of therapists' "nonspecific" personality factors (Frank, 1973; Gurman & Razin, 1977; Lambert, Shapiro, & Bergin, 1986), they prompt key questions about therapists' education and training (Bergin & Lambert, 1978; Garfield & Bergin, 1986). For if it is true that, "many . . . academic criteria . . . do not necessarily bear a direct relationship to skills in psychotherapeutic activities" (Garfield & Bergin, 1986, p. 11), or that therapists "may often be selected more for their academic credentials . . . than for their ability to relate and generate insights" (Bergin & Lambert, 1978, p. 150), then a serious reassessment of priorities is in order. The findings of this article reaffirm such a conclusion.

REFERENCES

Allen, T.W. (1967). Effectiveness of counselor trainees as a function of psychological openness. *Journal of Counseling Psychology 14*, 35-40.
Anastasi, A. (1976). *Psychological testing.* (4th ed.). New York: Collier Macmillan.
Aurbach, A. H. & Johnson, M. (1977). Research on the therapist's level of experience. In A.S. Gurman and A.M. Razin (Eds.), *Effective psychotherapy: A handbook of research* (pp. 84-102). New York: Pergamon Press Inc.
Bandura, A., Lipsher, D., & Miller, P.E. (1960). Psychotherapists' approach-avoidance reactions to patients' expressions of hostility. *Journal of Consulting Psychology, 24*, 1-8.
Bare, C.E. (1967). Relationship of counselor personality and client similarity to selected counseling success criteria. *Journal of Counseling Psychology, 14*, 419-425.

Bergin, A.E. (1966). Some implications of psychotherapy research for therapeutic practice. *Journal of Abnormal Psychology, 71*, 235-246.

Bergin, A.E. & Jasper, L.G. (1969). Correlates of empathy in psychotherapy: A replication. *Journal of Abnormal Psychology, 74*, 477-481.

Bergin, A.E. (1971). The evaluation of therapeutic outcomes. In A.E. Bergin and S.L. Garfield (Eds.), *Handbook of psychotherapy and behavior change: An empirical analysis* (pp. 217-270). New York: Wiley.

Bergin, A.E. & Lambert, M.J. (1978). The evaluation of 26 therapeutic outcomes. In A.E. Bergin and S.L. Garfield (Eds.), *Handbook of psychotherapy and behavior change:An empirical analysis* (pp. 139-190). New York: Wiley.

Beutler, L.E., Crago, M., & Arizmendi, T.G. (1986). Therapist variables in psychotherapy outcome and process. In S.L. Garfield and A. E. Bergin (Eds.), *Handbook of psychotherapy and behavior change* (pp. 257-310). New York: Wiley.

Buckley, D., Karasu, T.B., & Charles, E. (1981). Psychotherapists' personal therapy. *Psychotherapy: Theory, Research, & Practice. 18*, 299-305.

Bugental, J. F.T. (1976). *The search for existential identity.* San Francisco: Jossey-Bass.

Burton, A. (1972). *Twelve Therapists.* San Francisco: Jossey Bass.

Combs, A. W., & Soper, D.W. (1963). The perceptual organization of effective counselors. *Journal of Counseling Psychology, 10*, 222-226.

Creaser, J.W., & Carsello, C.J. (1979). Isolating factors related to paraprofessional effectiveness. *Journal of Counseling Psychology. 26*, 259-262.

Durlak, J.A. (1979). Comparative effectiveness of paraprofessional and professional helpers. *Psychological Bulletin, 86*, 80-92.

Ellsworth, S.G. The consistency of feeling-verbalization. *Journal of Counseling Psychology, 10*, 356-361.

Farber, B.A., & Heifitz, L. J. (1981). The satisfactions and stresses of psychotherapeutic work: A factor-analytic study. *Professional Psychology, 13*, 293-301.

Fiedler, F.E. (1950). The concept of an ideal therapeutic relationship. *Journal of Consulting Psychology, 14*, 239-245.

Fish, J.M. (1970). Empathy and the reported emotional experiences. *Journal of Consulting and Clinical Psychology, 35*, 61-64.

Foulds, M.L. Self-actualization and level of counselor interpersonal functioning. *Journal of Humanistic Psychology, 9*, (l), 87-92.

Frank, J.D. (1973). *Persuasion and healing: A comparative study of psychotherapy.* (rev. ed.) Baltimore: Johns Hopkins University Press.

Freud, S. (1958). Recommendations for physicians on the psycho-analytic method for treatment (1912). In J. Strachey (Ed. and Trans.), *The standard edition of the complete psychological works of Sigmund Freud*, Vol.12, pp.109-120, London: Hogarth Press. (Original work published in 1912).

Fromm-Reichman, F. (1950). *Principles of intensive psychotherapy.* Chicago: University of Chicago Press.

Garfield, S.L., & Bergin, A.E. (1971). Personal therapy, outcome and some therapist variables. *Psychotherapy: Theory, Research, & Practice, 8*, 251-253.

Garfield, S.L. & Bergin, A.E. (1986). Introduction and historical overview. In S.L. Garfield and A.E. Bergin (Eds.), *Handbook of psychotherapy and behavior change* (pp. 3-22). New York: Wiley.

Gibb, J.R. (1971). The effects of human relations training. In A.E. Bergin and S.L. Garfield (Eds.), *Handbook of psychotherapy and behavior change: An empirical analysis.* New York: Wiley & Sons.

Goodman, G. (1972). *Companionship therapy: Studies in structured intimacy.* San Francisco: Jossey Bass.

Gurman, A.S. (1972). Therapist mood patterns and therapeutic facilitation. *Journal of counseling Psychology, 19,* 169-170.

Gurman, A.S. (1977). The patient's perception of the therapeutic relationship. In A.S. Gurman & A.M. Razin (Eds.), *Effective psychotherapy: A handbook of research* (pp. 503-543). New York: Pergamon.

Gurman, A.S., & Razin, A.M. (Eds.) (1977). *Effective psychotherapy: A handbook of research.* New York: Pergamon Press.

Hellman, I.D., Morrison, T.L., & Abramowitz, S.I. (1987). Therapist experience and the stresses of psychotherapeutic work. *Psychotherapy: Theory, Research, & Practice, 24,* 171-177.

Holt, R.R., & Luborsky, L. (1958). *Personality patterns of psychiatrists,* Vols. 1 & 2. New York: Basic Books, Inc.

Jackson, M., & Thompson, C.L. (1971). Effective counselors' attitudes. *Journal of Counseling Psychology, 18,* 249-254.

Jourard, S.M. (1976). Changing personal worlds: A humanistic perspective. In A. Wandersman, P.J. Poppen, & D.F. Ricks (Eds.), *Humanism and behaviorism: Dialogue and growth* (pp. 35-53). New York: Pergamon Press.

Jung, C.G. (1964). The state of psychotherapy today. *Collected works* (Vol. 10, *Civilization in transition.)* Princeton, NJ: Princeton University Press. (Original work published 1934).

Laing, R.D. (1969). *Politics of the family.* New York: Vintage.

Lambert, M., Shapiro, D., & Bergin, A. (1986). The effectiveness of psychotherapy. In A. Bergin and S. Garfield (Eds.), *Handbook of psychotherapy and research* (pp. 157-212). New York: Wiley.

Lazarus, A. (1985). Setting the record straight. *American Psychologist, 40,* (12), 1418-1419.

Lorian, R.P., & Felner, R.D. (1986). Research on mental health with the disadvantaged. In S.L. Garfield & A.E. Bergin (Eds.), *Handbook of psychotherapy and behavior change* (pp. 739-775). New York: Wiley.

Luborsky, L., & Spence,D.P. (1978). Quantitative research on psychoanalytic therapy. In A.E. Bergin & S.L. Garfield (Eds.), *Handbook of psychotherapy and behavior change: An empirical analysis* (pp. 331-368). New York: Wiley.

Maslow, A.H. (1954). *Motivation and personality.* New York: Harper.

McConnaughy, E.A. (1987). The person of the therapist in psychotherapeutic practice. *Psychotherapy: Theory, Research, & Practice, 24,* 303-313.

McNair, D.M., Lorr, M., & Callahan, D.M. (1963). Patient and therapist influences on quitting psychotherapy. *Journal of Consulting Psychology 27*, 10-17.

McNair, D.M., Lorr, M., Young, H.H., Roth, I., & Boyd, R.W. (1964). A three year-follow-up of psychotherapy patients. *Journal of Clinical Psychology, 20*, 258-264.

Meltzoff, J., & Kornreich, M. (1970). *Research in psychotherapy.* New York: Atherton Press.

Oden, T. (1974). A populist's view of psychotherapeutic deprofessionalization. *Journal of Humanistic Psychology, 14*, 3-18.

Orlinsky, D.E. & Howard, K.I. (1978). The relation of process to outcome in psychotherapy. In A.E. Bergin & S.L. Garfield (Eds.), *Handbook of psychotherapy and behavior change: An empirical analysis* (pp. 283-330). New York: Wiley & Sons.

Parham, D., & Tinsley, H.E. (1980). What are friends for? Students' expectations of the friendship encounter. *Journal of Counseling Psychology, 27*, 524-527.

Parloff, M.B. (1956). Some factors affecting the quality of therapeutic relationships. *Journal of Abnormal Social Psychology, 52*, 5-10.

Parloff, M.B., Waskow, I.E.,& Wolf, B.E. (1978). Research on therapist variables in relation to process and outcome. In A.E. Bergin & S.L. Garfield (Eds.), *Handbook of psychotherapy and behavior change: An empirical analysis* (pp. 233-282). New York: Wiley & Sons.

Passon, W.R., & Olsen, L.C. (1969). Relation of counselor characteristics and empathic sensitivity. *Journal of Counseling Psychology, 16*, 440-445.

Peebles, M.J. (1980). Personal therapy and the ability to display empathy, warmth, and genuineness in psychotherapy. *Psychotherapy: Theory, Research, & Practice, 17*, 258-262.

Reik, T. (1948). Listening with the third ear: *The inner experience of a psychoanalyst.* New York: Farrar & Strauss.

Rogers, C.R. (1961). *On becoming a person.* Boston: Houghton Mifflin Co.

Rogers, C.R. (1980). *A way of being.* Boston: Houghton Mifflin Co.

Rowe, W., & Winborn, B.B. (1973). Self-actualization and counselor interpersonal functioning. *Journal of Humanistic Psychology, 13*, 79-84.

Sachs, H. (1947). Observations of a training analyst. *Psychoanalytic Quarterly, 16*, 157-168.

Schneider, K.J. (1984/1985). Clients' perceptions of the positive and negative characteristics of their counselors. (Doctoral dissertation, Saybrook Institute). *Dissertation Abstracts International, 45*, 3345B.

Shapiro, J.G., Krauss, H.H., & Truax, C.B. (1969). Therapeutic conditions and disclosure beyond the therapeutic encounter. *Journal of Counseling Psychology, 16*, 290-294.

Shapiro, J.G., & Voog, T. (1969). Effect of the inherently helpful person on student academic achievement. *Journal of Counseling Psychology, 16*, 505-509.

Smith, M.L., Glass, G.V., & Miller, T.I. (1980). *The benefits of psychotherapy.* Baltimore: Johns Hopkins University Press.

Stein, D.M., & Lambert, M.J. (1984). On the relationship between therapist experience and psychotherapy outcome. *Clinical Psychology Review, 4,* 127-142.

Strupp, H.H. (1955). Psychotherapeutic technique, professional affiliation, and experience level. *Journal of Consulting Psychology, 19,* 97-102.

Strupp, H.H. (1972). On the technology of psychotherapy. *Archives of General Psychiatry, 26,* 270-278.

Strupp, H.H., & Hadley, S.W. (1979). Specific vs. nonspecific factors in psychotherapy: A controlled study of outcome. *Archives of General Psychiatry, 36,* 1125-1136.

Truax, C.B., & Carkhuff, R.R. (1967). *Toward effective counseling and psychotherapy: Training and practice.* Chicago: Aldine.

Truax, C.B., & Mitchell, K.M. (1971). Research on certain therapist interpersonal skills in relation to process and outcome. In A.E. Bergin & S.L. Garfield (Eds.), *Handbook of psychotherapy and behavior change: An empirical analysis.* New York: Wiley.

Vandenbos, G.R., & Karon, B.P. (1971). Pathogenesis: A new therapist personality dimension related to therapeutic effectiveness. *Journal of Personality Assessment, 35,* 252-260.

Wogan, M. (1970). Effect of therapist-patient personality variables on therapeutic outcome. *Journal of Consulting Psychology, 35,* 356-361.

Psychotherapy and Redemption: A Tribute to a "Dying Mom"

Hendrika Vande Kemp

SUMMARY. In this case study, the author focuses on a victim of multiple abuse in her private life and of multiple violations illustrating how "helping" professionals become harmful and betray the trust implicit in psychotherapy. Details of the client's history are sketched, followed by a summary of the psychotherapeutic process; contacts with the ethics committee of the California Association of Marriage, Family, and Child Counselors; and the legal hearing by the Board of Behavioral Science Examiners of the Department of Consumer Affairs of the State of California. Most critical are the contacts between the client and supervisor since these hearings, which illustrate a reciprocal process of interpersonal influence and can be taken as representative of the redemptive life.

Wishing you . . .
    sunbeams dancing on your window,
    china bowls of blueberries and cream,
    A dozen really good new books,
    Afternoon tea with a special friend
    evening symphonies shared with someone you love,

Hendrika Vande Kemp, PhD, is Professor of Psychology at Fuller Theological Seminary, where her teaching duties have included courses on family therapy, family psychology, object relations theory, and domestic violence. Mailing address: Graduate School of Psychology, Fuller Theological Seminary, 180 N. Oakland Avenue, Pasadena, CA 91101.

This paper was presented at the 98th Annual Convention of the American Psychological Association at Boston, Tuesday August 14, 1990, at the invitation of Division 36, Psychologists Interested in Religious Issues, when the author received the William C. Bier Award.

93

peaceful nights of restoration . . .
Wishing you a year of meeting challenges,
fulfilling your goals and creating new dreams,
May God shower you with blessings
And be your constant companion.
Happy Birthday, Hendrika
("Deborah," 1979b)

I shall call her "Deborah," which is her given name. She has had a number of last names–her maiden name, two married names, a recent assumed name. The first three signify her role as property, her "belongingness" to abusive systems; each of these names is associated with a traumatic personal experience. Her *new name* signifies her new identity. Deborah denotes her separateness, the self who leaves Hell repeatedly; it is the place where she returns and finds a solid core of being. Deborah is a name well known to biblical scholars: She was a prophetess, one of the judges who helped the Israelites to freedom from the Canaanites (Judges 4-5). The name denotes "a bee" (Webster's, 1983). Deborah *is* like a bee: flying from flower to flower, cross-pollinating life's richness, creating connections between people that would not be there in her absence. Her *honey* is joy and gratitude.

FROM THEORETICAL PAPER TO CASE STUDY: A DECISION

When I was first notified that I would be the recipient of the William C. Bier award from Psychologists Interested in Religious Issues and was asked for a title for an invited address, I knew immediately that I wanted to speak on "Psychotherapy and Redemption," a topic that had been on my mind for some time (Vande Kemp, 1985, 1989; Vande Kemp & Houskamp, 1986), and was inspired by reading Count Igor Caruso's (1952/1964) *Existential psychology* and Wilfried Daim's (1953/1963) *Depth psychology and salvation*. My plans to present a theoretical paper based on their ideas were altered when I struggled to find the answer to a rhetorical question put to me by Deborah's caretaker:

You care–you really do even when you're hurting with sufferings of your own. You get little or no feedback from Deb and yet you continue to light up her day once a month with a little note and a check. Why are you so different? Rhetorical questions need no replies. But I still wonder about the anomalies–the breaks in the pattern, little points of light against a backdrop of blackness. Why do you care about a dying mom in Colorado, Hendrika? I suppose *that* you do is enough.[1]

My answer to him focused on Deborah, in a letter written to her that focused on her "gift of gratitude," a Christian "grace" described by Seward Hiltner (1972) in his *Theological Dynamics* (Ch. 2, "Grace and Gratitude"):

My answer to that would be very complex, and would involve many aspects of my faith. But all of that, even if elaborated for a hundred pages, would be only half of the answer; the other half is you, Deborah, and the person you are. I can only be honest and say that my life has been richly blessed by you. When I first came to know you, indirectly in supervision with Jeff, my first reaction was simply compassion for the intense emotional pain you were experiencing and anger at the sexual abuse. Eventually I became aware (still before meeting you) of a woman who had incredible grace and endurance despite extensive abuse. When I finally met you, I immediately felt your loving appreciation of both myself and Jeff: You had the ability to receive, which is one of the most significant components of the Kingdom of God. Many Christians mouth the platitude that "It is more blessed to give than to receive." There are surely ways that is true, but it is a dangerous generalization. In fact, it is possible to give *only* if there is someone willing to receive; and when someone receives what we have to give, whatever that giving may involve, that person affirms the acceptability-or "good-enoughness"–of what we have to give, and perhaps also of who we are.[2] (see also Vande Kemp, 1987)

In what follows, I will interweave Deborah's story with elements of my involvement with her and additional thoughts on redemption and psychotherapy.

DEBORAH: HER HISTORY

Deborah's current caretaker has written much of her early history (Rice, 1989). In an introduction to her story, he writes:

> This is Deborah's story. The story of a little girl lost in a grown-up world who was perpetually defiled and yet mysteriously retained her innocence. The things that happened to her would have shattered a lesser person beyond recognition. Though she brushed death many times, in her life the events had an entirely different effect.... Truth is a liberating thing to the heart that longs to possess it. This story is about the telling of truth in a life that has been abused by endless lies. (p. vi)

Deborah was the first-born of three children, and the only girl. That was her first existential error–to be born a girl. Deborah is one of many women receiving the message that femaleness is inferior, a message which leads to a peculiar kind of existential "sex guilt" that is described nowhere in the clinical literature.[3] Deborah learned quickly not to care about the lack of love, and at the age of four she vowed "she would never cry again," as screaming inevitably led to spanking and scolding. In relation to her abusive father, she created a secure defense:

> She was trapped inside a ball. Pastel colors in bands circled the globe. It was sunny outside and the sun's rays illumined the translucent rubber skin of the ball.... It wasn't bad being inside the ball if it weren't for being so alone. If only there was someone to play with inside the globe that entrapped her, she could have been happy.
> He was there without explanation. She didn't know how he got inside. His body was turned so that she couldn't see his

face. . . . As she approached he turned slowly toward her. Joy turned to terror. . . . His face was a blank. His eyes seemed to look beyond her. They were unfocused eyes, unseeing eyes, soulless eyes. That was it, they were eyes that allowed a seeing child to see into the inside of the man and behold only darkness. . . . He could get out, she could not. (pp. 2-3)

Her father was a violent man who spanked her, almost ritually, every night; this followed an equally ritual fight with her mother over an accusatory note Deborah would find under her pillow. In one violent episode he "shattered the door jamb and latch plate so that the door could never properly be closed again. . . . He never fixed the door. She was terrified to ask him to do so, [instinctively] knowing that in asking she would communicate her vulnerability," (Rice, 1989, p. 4) and thus forced to accept this violation of her boundaries. She endured the beatings to age 13, when she vowed her father would never touch her again. Later she recalled in her journals that this violence was sexually arousing, an insight which baffled and humiliated her. Sexuality in general was baffling: She received a little sex education in school, but was still caught off guard by her first menstrual period. Her mother's response was a lament that she was now a woman and could expect to experience an inordinate amount of pain for the rest of her life. She knew that her parents lacked affection, and that her mother hated sex, putting up with it out of a sense of duty. Thus, sexual confusion compounded the damage already inflicted by the existential sex guilt.

Adolescent dating experiences did little to prove her mother wrong; the interpersonal sexual reality constructed in these relationships did nothing to affirm Deborah's personhood (for a discussion of this issue, see Davis-Stephenson, 1989). Some dates were typically repressed and demanded little from her; others forced their attentions on her. Marty, a successful Christian law clerk, was her mother's favorite. But his behavior contradicted his strict Christian image, as he forced his attentions on her while parked on a mountain road. Deborah was frightened and asked him to stop, but only the appearance of a police cruiser rescued her. When she described this experience to her mother, her mother suggested that "she had imagined the whole thing or had caused him to become aroused by her provocative behavior" (Rice, 1989, p. 9).

Another evening Deborah "was confronted by a naked middle-aged man glaring at her" (Rice, 1989, p. 6). Her mother quickly disqualified this experience of indecent exposure (see Laing, 1965):

> Before Deborah had finished [her story], her mother dismissed what she was saying as a fabrication. She had made it up, it hadn't happened, and so there was no response that needed to be made.
>
> Deb's bearings began to waver. She had seen what her eyes had reported to her and had faithfully reported that to her mother in clear agitation. But rather than support and action, there was denial and accusation. Rather than something wrong in the world there was something wrong with the observer. It was her perceptions that were wrong, not wrong behavior that her perceptions had correctly recorded. . . .
>
> Something began to unravel in Deborah. Some vital link with reality and perception. Maybe things were not what they appeared to be after all, maybe there was other information not available to her that needed to be taken into account in order to construct an accurate model of the world. . . . Deborah was adrift on a sea of self-doubts . . . Who was this person after all who could so easily be doped into believing into existence things that never existed? (Rice, 1989, pp. 6-7)

Thus were sown the seeds of problems in reality testing, the roots of hallucinations and psychosis. As Watzlawick (1976) states in *How Real is Real?*: "If an individual is punished for correct perception of the outside world or of [the] self by a significant other (e.g., a child by a parent), [s]he will learn to distrust the data of [her] own senses" (p. 18; see also Watzlawick, Beavin, & Jackson, 1967). This is what R. D. Laing (1965) described as *mystification,* which "induces confusion in the sense that there is a failure to see what is 'really' being experienced, or being done, or going on, and failure to distinguish or discriminate the actual issues" (p. 344; see also the discussion of invalidation in Laing, 1969).

By the time of Deborah's first marriage, she was confused enough not to know whether or not she loved her husband, or even to wonder why. How damaging this was to her became clear on her wedding night: They were both virgins, and when her husband attempted penetration they found that "the door was closed and he could not get in" (p. 14). On the second night of the honeymoon she was raped, bleeding, and beaten until "her buttocks were numb." Deborah had, unwittingly, "married her father": She again was subject to beatings and the attribution that this is what women liked. He had invaded the ball where she was trapped: "She would be there the next time he chose to come in" (Rice, 1989, p. 15). When she went for medical help, she found no comfort:

[The doctor] confirmed what she already supposed. She had ripped and torn. He advised a six-week abstinence from sex while she healed. Incredibly, he went on to admonish her for not trying hard enough at relaxing. This was all very confusing to her. Language wasn't intended to be used like this. How do you try hard to relax? (p. 17)

Unknowing, Deborah identified the "be spontaneous paradox," which occurs "whenever somebody demands of another person behavior that by its very nature must be spontaneous but now cannot be because it is demanded" (Watzlawick, 1976, p. 19). Deborah's questioning was also a gift of grace, allowing her to cling to sanity despite the nearly irresistible pull to succumb to insanity (see Laing & Esterson, 1970).

Deborah wanted to make her marriage work. But in 4 years she had successful intercourse only twice, after having her genitals dilated and anesthetized—in essence, she had to be physically numb. Her sexual failure was humiliating in a Christian subculture that valued marriage above all else, and considered divorce a great sin—much greater than the sins of physical, sexual, verbal, and psychological abuse (for an exploration of these abuse categories, see Rodenburg, 1990). Her husband forced her to wear clothes that would transform her into the sex object he desired, and he enrolled her in a therapeutic process that ended in a nightmare.

DEBORAH: THE THERAPEUTIC NIGHTMARE

I first heard of Deborah in the Fall of 1978, when her case was presented to me for supervision by a practicum student. She was referred to our clinic by a local pastor, and had since 1971 been under the care of six different therapists. In 1976 she had been hospitalized for 2 months after a suicide attempt that followed a relationship crisis–cutting herself was a frequent form of self-abuse between 1971 and 1976. Treatment continued with a variety of drugs for the next several years: Moban, Loxitane, Mellaril, Elavil, Valium, Benadryl, Nembutal, and Lithium Carbonate. Later, a gift of grace was the psychiatrist who took her off all psychotropic drugs and supervised her treatment of diet and exercise.

During 1975 and 1976 Deborah experienced a severe food phobia. In 1977 she was severely anorexic; by Christmas her weight had dropped 60 pounds to 97 pounds. She experienced auditory and visual hallucinations. The psychiatric history gathered by 1978 included diagnoses of depressive neurosis, manic-depressive psychosis, schizo-affective reaction, and conversion reaction. Our observations at various times justified all these diagnoses, and pointed clearly to a major personality disorder with schizoid, schizotypal, and borderline elements. During the first few months of therapy she experienced conversion symptoms such as parathesia of the limbs and trunk, myoparesis, and tachycardia. She was a definite suicide risk, having made at least 20 previous attempts and continuing to make frequent threats and gestures (additional details of the case are summarized in "Deborah," 1979a; J. W., 1979; Rice, 1989; Vande Kemp, 1981).

A baffling clinical puzzle was set when Deborah described the 14 characters who comprised her fantasy life. She did not suffer from a dissociative disorder, but the fantasy had the strength of a delusional system. The characters were people who talked to, influenced, persecuted, encouraged, and represented the diverse aspects of Deborah's personality. In a paper she wrote for her therapist, she described these characters and addressed them as follows: "Do any of you have anything to say to me? I'm fragmenting–and sinking in despair. Will you sign my certificate of life with meaning or one of death[?]–for without the first the last will surely follow." Her personalities then voted. It was a close vote: 6 for living, 7 for dying, 1 "on the fence." One of the characters promised to torment her because she was "so incredibly disgusting, repulsive, wretched, and decrepit" (J. W., 1979).

We were dismayed to discover that Deborah had been sexually abused by two of her Christian therapists–one a clinical psychologist who had since moved out of state, the second a Marriage, Family, and Child Counselor (MFCC). When she entered therapy with the MFCC, she was grieving the loss of the psychologist (who moved away but promised to return) and the loss of her marriage. Therapy appears to have been laden with sexual overtones: Her journal entries for these months reflect not only a great deal of emphasis on her sexuality during the therapy sessions, but also the fact that she filled a two-month's prescription for birth control pills. The MFCC confronted her continually about her sexual rigidity, and encouraged her–as had her husband–to wear tight pants, sexier bras, more flattering shoes that would make her legs look sexy. He felt that her anorexic body was very sexy.

While the therapist kept the focus on sexual issues, Deborah's journal entries reflected feelings of intense despair and ever-present suicidal ideation and gestures. She cut herself almost daily, and suffered a great deal of pain from the cuts to her arms and legs. All food except milk was promptly regurgitated. She was so cold that she spent most of her time curled up with blankets and quilts and wore warm sweaters and coats to work while others went sleeveless. Heavy doses of Valium helped her sleep; she wished she could take enough to die.

Shortly after she began this treatment, she consulted a psychiatrist about her medication. Learning who her therapist was, he informed her that the MFCC had been accused of sexual misconduct by a former patient. He did not, however, raise legitimate questions of the MFCC's competence to see someone with Deborah's diagnosis, even though he was clearly practicing outside the bounds of the MFCC license as defined by current California law. When Deborah confronted the MFCC about the charge, he denied it–she wanted it not to be true; she needed to trust him and was transferentially "in love" with him. She felt that her questioning alone had hurt him, and that she needed to apologize. Yet she was so afraid of communicating her real feelings to him directly that she let "Lisa," one of her 14 fantasy characters, make the journal entries.

In December of 1977 the MFCC began to "reparent" Deborah. She would bring her blanket with her to therapy, and he would hold her and stroke her. Late one evening, after having had a session at 8:00 p.m., he appeared at her apartment unannounced, carrying a bottle of sherry and approaching her sexually. She assumed that "he knew what he was doing, that he was trying to help me, trying to do me a favor." It was painful for her, but he kept telling her that the pain would be over soon, and to her surprise she found herself orgasmic. A day or two later the psychologist (and previous therapist) also visited her apartment. Two more incidents occurred with the MFCC before he was injured in a car accident, which only increased Deborah's desire to care for him and not hurt him further. She was ready to do anything he asked, as long as it would not lead him to reject her–dynamics typical of incest victims. She continued in therapy for the next several months, with most of the therapy sessions scheduled in the late evening or on the weekends. There were about 20 addition sexual encounters–7 of them in his office–which involved intercourse as well as oral and anal sex. He continued to visit her at her apartment, and stressed the importance of her commitment to him. She took this commitment as seriously as marriage, and it was one of the factors that made it extremely difficult for her to bring charges against him. Yet she knew that therapy was not helping her, and at her instigation she terminated the treatment. She found herself possessed of a strength and an observing ego–gifts of grace–that defied all the lies and betrayal offered under the guise of therapy.

DEBORAH: MY PILGRIMAGE INTO SISTERHOOD

Obviously, Deborah's case presented a difficult challenge to my practicum student, and it was necessary for me to become involved in her case in ways that exceeded the usual requirements of supervision. I began as another therapist, familiar with her case, whom she could call in an emergency. It took Deborah about 4 months to decide to initiate charges against the MFCC–the decision came only after she realized that other women were vulnerable to the same transference reactions she had, and the therapist's inability to process these appropriately. Thus, her own salvation came out of her concern for others.

Our initial action was to file charges with the ethics committee of the California Association of Marriage, Family, and Child Counselors (CAMFCC). On the occasions when Deborah had to meet with the committee and needed her therapist's support and company, I accompanied them so that they could not be subject to accusations of impropriety. My decision was based purely on an assessment of possible risk, as her therapist responded to her emotional age of around 2 years: In his own words, "she was a child," and there was absolutely nothing seductive in her behavior. His maturity and insight was another gift of grace; few students are gifted with such discernment and ability "to contain."

The ethics committee investigated the case and determined that Deborah's therapist was guilty of ethical violations, and demanded that he seek approved supervision and personal psychotherapy. They also felt that their power was limited; he could escape it by resigning from CAMFCC. They recommended that we file charges with the Board of Behavioral Science Examiners (BBSE) and advised us that action was more likely to result if we sent a copy of the complaint to Governor Brown's office, because of his deep concern about violations of this nature–surely one of the "graces" of the Brown administration. We followed this advice, and were gratified that BBSE immediately pursued the case. The chair of the board attended the hearing, which was one of the first cases of client sexual abuse by a therapist prosecuted by BBSE, to observe the procedures and assure BBSE that it was handled properly (as a "test case"). Again, I accompanied Deborah and her therapist to initial meetings with the deputy from the Attorney General's Office and the later trial. Since she was the major witness, she was not allowed into the courtroom except when she was called in to testify. We decided that her current therapist should function as our courtroom observer, and I would stay with her for the emotional support she needed, which was not available from her family or church. The price of this was that all three of us were victims of harassing phone calls, and Deborah and her therapist both had their tires slashed during a therapy session. The hearing resulted in the removal of the therapist's license (see Cameron, 1980; for current California standards, see Quinn, 1990).

Throughout these months of ethical and legal hearings, I of course came to know Deborah very well, taking on the role of a concerned older sister or parent. I was able to observe that my student's interactions with her were indeed appropriate, and that her behavior "pulled for" nothing more than therapeutic empathy and "Christian compassion."

Two weeks after the BBSE hearings, Deborah was brutally assaulted while jogging, in an attack that was neither intended robbery nor rape. Although she did not require hospitalization, the social worker at the emergency room did not want her to go home to be alone, and asked her whom she could call. Feeling (I think quite accurately) that her mystifying mother would simply accuse her of "causing" the attack, she called me. At that point I certainly responded out of Christian compassion rather than a review of the ethical principles governing dual-role relationships. I scrounged in my closets for something Deborah could wear, and drove to the emergency room. We picked up additional clothes and personal grooming items at her apartment, and I took her home with me, where she stayed for the weekend. I remember this weekend vividly: It was Thanksgiving, and a friend and I prepared a holiday dinner for Deborah and another friend who had had recent surgery for a brain tumor; the four of us went to see *Fiddler on the Roof.* I made several trips with Deborah back to her apartment, and assured myself that she could handle being alone there. This experience was, of course, somewhat confusing to Deborah, as she had had a certain amount of transference to me as a "good-enough mother," and it was difficult suddenly to confront the reality of my personal life–a good argument against dual-role relationships. These issue were resolved with her therapist.

At that point, whatever responses Deborah had to me were genuine (rather than transferential) feelings of gratitude to someone who had befriended her. During the therapy process she sent me several appreciative notes. These were appropriate, as the time and energy required of me were definitely "above and beyond" the normal duties of a supervisor, and of course could not be paid for in any way. At one point she presented me with a lovely hand-made birthday card–she was gifted artistically and supported herself as a graphic artist (over the years all her Christmas cards have been personally designed, as were her wedding invitations and birth announcements). When she was married, she made a trip to campus just to share her happiness and joy with me. After all the pathology and misery I had seen in the past, it was important for her to share the positive developments in her life.

Deborah eventually moved out of the area, but kept in touch through her annual Christmas letter, and invited me to visit. I spent Christmas with friends in the area in 1985, and took the time to visit Deborah and her family. She was married to an ambitious young Christian professional, and had recently given birth to her second child. She appeared to be happy in motherhood, and described her husband to me as loving and patient with her sexual fears. She also shared that she had recently been diagnosed with breast cancer, that they had decided to treat it "organically," and that all was going well. I had some concerns about this, but didn't feel that it was my place to challenge the decision, especially since she appeared healthy and thriving.

In 1986 the couple moved out of state, and I again received their Christmas letters and notice of the birth of their third child in 1987. Christmas 1988 came and went, with no letter from Deborah–I noticed this omission, and was a little curious and concerned. Early in 1989 I received a letter from a couple in the out-of-state town where she lived. They were neighbors who had come to know her through a church group, and had for a variety of reasons become concerned about her emotional and physical health. They soon discovered that her husband had refused to allow medical treatment for the breast cancer, and her breast had literally been consumed. This couple, the parents of three small children, persuaded her to leave the husband, took her and the children into their own home, and began to arrange for her medical treatment. An oncologist was persuaded to donate treatment for the cancer which had metastasized into the bone, and the hospital also provided some free services.

This couple wrote to me, as one of Deborah's "friends," asking if I could help out financially. I was of course deeply concerned, and established through a conversation with her brother that her illness was indeed life-threatening and the need for support very real. At that point I decided–as a "fellow Christian" and friend, that I would commit myself to some financial support, but that I also wanted to verify the details of the situation for myself. I was traveling to the area on business in June and arranged to visit Deborah and her "adopted family." Sharing with them in a morning of family life and a luncheon, I was satisfied that this couple were indeed loving, caring parents and friends, and were acting from true "Christian" motives. I made a second visit as well, since Deborah was in frail health as a result of radiation and chemotherapy. At the end of this visit, Deborah and the children were on the way to see the social worker appointed by the courts to assess her request for custody, and she asked if I would be willing to speak to the social worker. I spoke to her later last summer–in my role as therapist/supervisor–and Deborah was awarded custody despite her terminal illness. I believe that her ex-husband's emotional abuse and neglect were also significant factors.

At this point, her death is imminent, and the couple with whom she is living are hoping to gain custody of the children. I will do all that I can to support their request, in my professional role and as a family friend. In the few minutes remaining to me, I want to answer the question that may now be on your lips: How did the role of a deeply disturbed client become transformed into that of "sister and friend"? What factors in our relationship constituted it as redemptive?

The Redemptive Therapist "Binds Together"

One of the meanings of religion is, "literally, a reconnection, reunion, reconciliation" (Mowrer, 1966, p. 37). Viktor Frankl (1975) applied this directly to the therapy process: The client struggles "to be 'connected' again, to be 're-connected'" (p. 75). Fritz Künkel (1954) stated that "the client is separated from his real life, divorced from reality . . . cut off from God" (pp. 5-6). The Christ-like therapist facilitates such reconnection. In Deborah's case, significant reconnections with reality were reinforced by the rulings of the CAMFCC and the BBSE.

The Redemptive Therapist Affirms the Longing for Salvation

Caruso (1952/1964) asserts that our clients manifest a strong "drive for salvation and for the Christ-archetype" (p. 11). The therapist must fit in some way the client's Christ-archetype, as an embodiment and channel for God's grace. In this way, the therapist facilitates *metanoia,* "the biblical word for change of mind and heart" (White, 1952, p. 146). In Deborah's transformation from "deeply disturbed client" to bride and mother and friend–free of psychological symptoms–we see this process of *metanoia.*

The Redemptive Therapist Recognizes Her Own Limits

The therapist recognizes the boundary between her human, finite self and the Christ-archetype she embodies. Both Caruso (1952/1964) and Daim (1953/1963) warn against confusing the psychotherapy process with true salvation and the therapist with Christ. Caruso (1952/1964) notes that countertransference connected with the Christ-archetype is even more dangerous than sexual countertransference. In this case, Deborah's early therapists displayed an arrogance that clearly reflects a lack of awareness of the limitations of their role, defying this rule. Her student therapist struggled with this temptation and resisted it:

> Within the first three months of therapy, I learned that any thought of being this woman's "savior" was totally inappropriate. She was too needy; I could never give enough to make her better. Perhaps this was a good way to learn this lesson early in my career. That is, it was probably better to be overwhelmed by someone who, I had to admit, was beyond my rescue, than to fool myself by "saving" countless souls over the years who might indeed appear to be easier candidates for "saving." (J. W., 1979, pp. 31-32)

Redemptive Therapy Releases from Heresy

Caruso (1952/1964) regarded neurosis as "existential heresy." Daim (1953/1963) noted that "the normal tendency of acknowledging the true absolute–the transcendental God–is repressed and something relative is endowed with absolute character" (p. 26), echoing Paul Tillich's (1957) definition of sin: "in idolatrous faith preliminary, finite realities are elevated to the rank of ultimacy" (p. 12). Deborah was encouraged in such idolatry by a therapist who allowed her to worship him, forcing her to make a unilateral, life-long commitment. Deborah could not begin her transformation until she violated this idolatrous commitment and recognized her therapist's potential for evil.

The Redemptive Therapist Manifests "Agape"

William Rickel (1956) noted that therapy must lead to a point at which the client can say: "I have a strong feeling and certitude that there is some gracious power outside myself that loves me and has accepted me" (p. 83). Doris Mode (1956) noted that the miraculous element in psychotherapy is "the re-establishment of relationship to God, even though another human stirs this into being because [s]he too has the same divine spark and is willing to use it in the interest of serving God–for the patient's release" (pp. 51-52). Deborah found these qualities in both her therapist and her supervisor, and manifested the gratitude that flows forth in response to the movement of God's grace.

The Redemptive Therapist Affirms God's Creation

Deborah has been a witness to God's grace for all of us, but it took her many years to accept herself. A gratifying result of her therapist's gentle but persistent confrontation and reality testing was the switch in her writing: At first all references to herself would be in the lower case "i," because "she did not deserve to capitalize herself" (J. W., 1979, p. 17). Once she had launched her case with the BBSE, Deborah wrote an open letter to her abusive former therapists that she regarded as a "hymn of rededication" (p. 27). She no longer blamed herself for her misfortunes and was taking control of her life. In this letter, "the 'I's were all capitalized because she said she realized that she matters as an 'I' in God's creation, not as an 'i'" (p. 28).

NOTES

1. Virgil F. Rice to Hendrika Vande Kemp, 22 April 1990, p. 4.
2. Hendrika Vande Kemp to Deborah, 18 May 1990, pp. 2-3.
3. For several years the concept of existential sex guilt has intrigued me as a way to understand the development of many "normal" women and special concerns presented by female clients, one of whom spoke of looking in the mirror and "not seeing myself." For her, her body provided no protection for her fragile sense of self.

An analysis of what I have come to understand as *existential sex guilt* might follow the analysis laid down by Paul Tillich (1952), in *The Courage to Be*, for the threats to being. *Nonbeing* threatens our existence from three different directions: It threatens our *"ontic self-affirmation,* relatively in terms of fate, absolutely in terms of death;" it threatens our *"spiritual* self-affirmation, relatively in terms of emptiness, absolutely in terms of meaninglessness;" it threatens our *"moral self-affirmation,* relatively in terms of guilt, absolutely in terms of condemnation" (p. 41 for all quotes; italics added). Tillich points out that anxiety about fate and death, emptiness and loss of meaning, and guilt and condemnation, are part of the existential givenness of human existence, though each has a neurotic as well as a "human" version.

One could also conduct this analysis using the classic psychological and theological classifications of guilt as *real, neurotic, false,* or *existential.* At an *existential* level, sex guilt is guilt over one's *embodiment.* Applying Laing's concept of mystification, the message "you should not be" applies to one's embodiment. This may lead to a fear of being disembodied but somehow continuing to exist, or of having to exist in a sexually neutral state.

REFERENCES

Cameron, K. (1980). In the matter of the accusation against *Larry Dean Faulkner.* Sacramento, CA: Board of Behavioral Science Examiners, Department of Consumer Affairs, State of California.

Caruso, I. (1964). *Existential psychology: From analysis to synthesis* (E. Krapf, Trans.). New York: Herder & Herder (Original work published 1952).

Daim, W. (1963). *Depth psychology and salvation* (K. F. Reinhardt, Trans.). New York: Frederick Ungar (Original work published 1953).

Davis-Stephenson, C. (1989). *The construction of childhood sexuality: A symbolic interactionist perspective.* Unpublished doctoral dissertation, Graduate School of Psychology, Fuller Theological Seminary, Pasadena, CA.

"Deborah." (1979a). *Untitled summary of events.* Unpublished manuscript, Pasadena, CA.

"Deborah." (1979b). *Untitled poem.* Unpublished poem, Pasadena, CA.

Frankl, V. (1975). *The unconscious god: Psychotherapy and theology.* New York: Simon & Schuster.

Hiltner, S. (1972). *Theological dynamics*. Nashville: Abingdon.

J. W. (1979). Untitled case summary. Pasadena Community Counseling Clinic.

Künkel, F. (1954). The integration of psychology and religion. *Journal of Psychotherapy as a Religious Process, 1*, 1-11.

Laing, R. D. (1965). Mystification, confusion, and conflict. In I. Boszormenyi-Nagy and J. L. Framo (Eds.), *Intensive family therapy: Theoretical and practical aspects* (pp. 343-363). New York: Harper & Row.

Laing, R. D. (1969). *The politics of the family and other essays*. New York: Random House/Pantheon.

Laing, R. D., & Esterson, A. (1970). *Sanity, madness and the family: Families of schizophrenics* (2nd ed.). London: Tavistock.

Mode, D. (1956). A psychoanalytic view of miracles. *Journal of Psychotherapy as a Religious Process, 3*, 47-52.

Mowrer, O. H. (1966). *Abnormal reactions or actions? (An auto-biographical answer)*. Dubuque, IA: Wm. C. Brown.

Quinn, V. (1990). *Professional therapy never includes sex*. Sacramento, CA: Department of Consumer Affairs/Office of State Printing.

Rice, V. R. (1989). *A cry from the dark: A collection of stories*. Unpublished manuscript, Boulder, CO.

Rickel, W. (1956). Concepts of power in personality as seen by Otto Rank and Reinhold Niebuhr. *Journal of Psychotherapy as a Religious Process, 3*, 77-91.

Rodenburg, F. (1990). *Quantifying wife abuse: Development of the Wife Abuse Measure (WAM)*. Unpublished doctoral dissertation, Graduate School of Psychology, Fuller Theological Seminary, Pasadena, CA.

Tillich, P. (1952). *The courage to be*. New Haven: Yale University Press.

Tillich, P. (1957). *The dynamics of faith*. New York: Harper & Row.

Vande Kemp, H. (1981). *When "helping" professionals become harmful*. Unpublished case study, Graduate School of Psychology, Fuller Theological Seminary, Pasadena, CA.

Vande Kemp, H. (1985). *Psychotheological integration in the 1950s: The Journal of Psychotherapy as a Religious Process*. Paper presented at the meeting of the American Psychological Association in Los Angeles, August 1985; at the American Academy of Religion in Anaheim, CA, November 1985; and at the Eastern region of the Christian Association for Psychological Studies, Lancaster, PA, October 1987.

Vande Kemp, H. (1987). Relational ethics in the novels of Charles Williams. *Family Process, 26*(2), 283-294.

Vande Kemp, H. (1989). *Redemption and psychotherapy*. Unpublished paper presented to the Joint Faculty of Fuller Theological Seminary, Pasadena, CA.

Vande Kemp, H., & Houskamp, B. M. (1986). An early attempt at integration: *The Journal of Psychotherapy as a Religious Process. Journal of Psychology and Theology, 14*(1), 3-14.

Watzlawick, P. (1976). *How real is real? Confusion, disinformation, communication*. New York: Random House/Vintage Books.

Watzlawick, P., Beavin, J. H., & Jackson, D. C. (1967). *Pragmatics of human communication: A study of interactional patterns, pathologies, and paradoxes.* New York: W. W. Norton & Co.

Webster's new universal unabridged dictionary, 2nd ed., (1983). New York: Simon and Schuster.

White, V. F. (1952). *God and the unconscious.* Cleveland: World.

Betrayed
Within the Therapeutic Relationship:
An Integrity Therapy Perspective

Nedra R. Lander
Danielle Nahon

SUMMARY. This paper presents an Integrity Therapy perspective on ways in which traditional humanistic and analytic therapies can entrap both therapist and patient into a betrayal of self and the relationship. Through the use of clinical anecdotes, nuances in the therapeutic betrayal of the patient are examined with respect to the power differential in the therapeutic relationship and the concept of value clashes between therapist and client versus psychopathological explanations of therapeutic impasses. Finally, the ways in which current training models can create a betrayal of future patient/client relationships will be examined.

"Betrayal" is defined in the Concise Oxford Dictionary as a state of being disloyal to, to lead one astray, or to reveal treacherously

Nedra R. Lander, PhD, C.Psych., is a graduate of the University of Illinois, receiving much of her training from C.H. Patterson and O. Hobart Mowrer. Her work with Mowrer introduced her to the concept of Integrity Therapy, an approach which she has continued to develop and share with others.

Dr. Lander has worked as a senior psychologist at the Ottawa Civic Hospital since 1975. Mailing address: Department of Psychiatry, CPC3, Ottawa Civic Hospital, 1053 Carling Ave., Ottawa, Ontario, Canada, K1Y 4E9.

Danielle Nahon, MA, has been employed as a senior psychotherapist at the Ottawa Civic Hospital since 1979. She is a Doctoral Candidate in Psychology at the University of Montreal, with a research specialty in the field of gender role psychotherapy for men. Mailing address: Department of Psychiatry, CPC3, Ottawa Civic Hospital, 1053 Carling Ave., Ottawa, Ontario, Canada, K1Y 4E9.

The authors would like to thank Mr. Stephen West for his generous editorial assistance in the preparation of this manuscript.

113

and involuntarily. "Loyalty" is defined as being true, faithful to duty, love, or obligation. The concepts of loyalty and betrayal are critical ones for the therapist to examine. A client who enters into a psychotherapeutic relationship, enters into a sacred trust. In addition to the overt obligation to be loyal to the code of ethical practice of a given mental health discipline, the therapist also enters into an unspoken, moral contract of loyalty to treat the client with human dignity, and to offer a treatment which will enhance the client's personal empowerment in reaching a higher level of mental health and of resolving his or her difficulties with living. The existence of ethical rules of conduct strives to ensure that a betrayal of the client along such overt parameters of fees charged, lack of sexual involvement with the therapist, confidentiality, and so on will not take place. Our focus in this paper will not be on this more overt form of betrayal, but rather on a more covert and insidious betrayal which occurs within the implicit contract of providing empowerment to the client.

We would like to develop the thesis that, inadvertently, traditional psychotherapies frequently lead to an involuntary betrayal of the client by virtue of the conceptualization of what constitutes mental illness and what is necessary in order for an individual to recover or reclaim mental health. Through the use of clinical anecdotes drawn from our work as psychotherapists in a large tertiary-care teaching hospital setting, we will explore the theme of betrayal of the client in the therapist-client relationship from the standpoint of its built-in integrity or lack thereof. The theoretical perspective we will use is that of Integrity Therapy. Focusing on the areas of the power differential in the therapeutic relationship, the implications of positive regard, the use of empathy and self-disclosure, as well as the concept of value clashes between therapist and client versus psychiatric labelling, we will explore the ways in which traditional humanistic and analytic therapies can entrap both therapist and patient into a betrayal of self and of the relationship.

INTEGRITY THERAPY

Integrity Therapy, a concept first coined by O. Hobart Mowrer (1936,1964), purports that mental illness stems from the individual's lack of integrity with both self and others. Mowrer had come to appreciate that his own as well as others' "difficulties in life and with living" stemmed not from intrapsychic conflicts but rather from interpersonal conflicts in which they were participants. In radical contrast with the Freudian perspective of guilt as stemming from a victimization of the ego by an oversocialized superego, Mowrer viewed guilt as a healthy response of the ego to the inner awareness of dishonest or deceitful behaviors toward oneself and others. The neurotic, in Mowrer's (1953, 1954) view, therefore suffers not from the dread of what he or she will or might do, but from a well-justified fear of the social consequences of deeds already done. In Mowrer's view, what psychotherapy calls for is not new or different values, but rather a greater fidelity or integrity to one's present value system. Therefore, a befitting descriptor for this approach is that of "Integrity Therapy" (Mowrer, 1938). Pivotal to Integrity Therapy is a reformulation of the importance of guilt, moral conscience, and the possibility for social reintegration through making amends. Of further importance is the re-conceptualization of the therapist-client relationship as based on the three principles of Integrity Therapy–honesty, responsibility, and increased emotional involvement with others.

If the therapeutic relationship is to be real and bona fide, and therefore a truly "corrective emotional experience" in Alexander's term (1946), it behooves not only the patient but also the therapist to adhere to these guidelines of interpersonal behavior. It is our view that the behavior of the therapist as it is defined by the traditional psychotherapies, although well intentioned and guided by "sound" and/or empirical principles, may inadvertently set up both the therapist and the therapeutic situation for an insidious or covert disempowerment and subsequent betrayal of the patient.

THE POWER DIFFERENTIAL
IN THE THERAPEUTIC RELATIONSHIP

The demands which Integrity Therapy makes on the therapist to be as open as the client about the "secrets" in his or her past and present result in a unique power equality between therapist and client. Quite simply, Integrity Therapy insists that within the therapeutic relationship, one must not ask others to do something which one is not willing to do oneself, for example, to self-disclose. This removes the couch, desk, and highback chair from within the therapeutic relationship, allowing instead for an encounter between two human beings, both daring to own their human foibles and their accountabilities.

Although this perspective may sound reflective of the basic tenets of the humanistic theories in which the therapist is encouraged to be more "humanistic" within the therapeutic encounter, there are a number of fundamental differences between Integrity Therapy and all other theories with respect to the therapist-client relationship. From our studies and our dialogues with other professionals, it appears to us that the choice of words and the images portrayed frequently reveal the presence of a hierarchical split between therapist and client. For example, in examining the three pillars of client-centred therapy–positive regard, empathy, and self-disclosure–from the perspective of the therapist-client relationship, we note the following differences.

1. With Respect to the Need for Positive Regard

In our view, the positive acceptance of the client no matter what his or her behaviors results in a fundamentally fraudulent relationship. Every therapist *does* at times hold definite feelings toward the behavior of the client. Therefore, to forbid the therapist from insisting on a minimal standard of behavior from the client is to force one to behave without integrity, thereby disempowering the client by implying that one is incapable of better behavior. This comprises a betrayal of the other, in that it reinforces the creation of memory traces for the client of having engaged in interpersonally destructive and therefore self-loathing behavior.

To allow and even encourage the client to act out within the therapeutic encounter comprises a collusion with the client's psychopathology. For example, if the therapist sits back passively as the client acts out by throwing books about the office, or if the therapist encourages the client to express anger by pounding a pillow, or accepts the client unconditionally as he or she engages in a sexual rampage on the town as a rage response (toward either the therapist or another individual) rather than challenging the client to find more honorable or personally acceptable ways of handling this anger with active creative control, there is a betrayal of the client's capacity to put a stop to old destructive patterns of behavior.

From our experience, it is much more therapeutic for the therapist to clearly draw a boundary by declaring his or her values and boundaries regarding what is acceptable versus non-acceptable behavior in the therapist's value system; it provides the clients with a "real" relationship, whereby they can begin to differentiate their own value system. It is difficult to differentiate and grow in a vacuum. It is the very vacuum created by the therapist neutrality in analytically oriented therapies which generates abandonment anxieties and the defences against them. It is within the transference relationship with a clearly defined therapist that the client can begin to differentiate from the therapist. To withhold the therapist's self-disclosure within the therapeutic relationship comprises a betrayal of the patient, who is so desperate to find out who he or she is, and can only do this while colliding with the other's boundaries and learning the "me" versus the "not me" in resisting the pull for fusion or splitting as defenses against the existential abyss.

2. With Regard to the Therapeutic Use of Empathy

We have found that more often than not empathy in real practice becomes sympathy, implying a power imbalance. Furthermore, we have repeatedly noted amongst other therapists an explicit and determined focus on delving into the pain or suffering in the client's past. In contrast, the focus of Integrity Therapy is to challenge those *behaviors* that have caused the distressing feelings in the first place. From the Integrity perspective, to make the expression of repressed pain be the focus of therapy is to set up the client for an insidious and covert disempowerment and subsequent betrayal in the following ways: First, this sets up the client to remain in a victim frame, whereby others, or one's unfortunate circumstances, or one's tragic past, or one's repressed emotions form the basis for mental illness. This perspective legitimizes the client's avoidance of having to undergo the painful process of uncovering and fixing up the fraudulent interpersonal patterns in past and present behaviors that have contributed to the etiology and maintenance of the "pain." Over the years, we have observed that this focus on pain has led the therapist to adopt an attitude of increased and accentuated *sympathy* for the client's victimization, which then leads the therapist to become more "gentle and nurturing," and thus less likely to challenge the client in a more "tough love" style to examine the integrity violations underlying the "pain" which he or she is experiencing. Consonant with this is the observation of the parallel response of some "feeling-oriented" therapists to the integrity challenge, as being "judgmental." This challenge implies the view that to call someone else's behavior into question comprises a betrayal. However, the Integrity approach purports that to overtly sanction the client's fraudulent behaviors by *not* challenging their lack of integrity is to betray the client. In actual practice, these therapists tend to remain gentle and nurturing as long as the client is cooperative in "showing feelings," especially "tears," in response to the therapeutic interventions. However, if the client "withholds feelings," this seems to legitimize the therapist's becoming overtly hostile and confrontive, thus betraying the client. Of interest, in a number of cases where we have worked with individuals in psychotherapy who had undergone this type of experience with previous therapists, we subsequently discovered that the pain that our clients had experienced through their tears in fact was a rage response to the violation inherent in the history-taking or therapeutic process whereby their pain was "uncovered" and "experienced."

We are particularly concerned with the potential betrayal of the client inherent in the existing training models for mental health professionals. For example, within the context of a teaching-hospital environment, the model of bed-to-bed teaching rounds is frequently utilized. Here, the patient is interviewed by a team, often consisting of staff therapists as well as students of varying ranks. In the context of this interview, it is often not only fair game, but often the requirement for both staff and student to demonstrate the use of those techniques which can "work" in getting the client to emote and furthermore to elicit meaningful personal historical material. One such client, after being interviewed in this fashion, had to work hard in individual therapy to begin to validate her sense of betrayal and violation by this process. She had naturally assumed that because her interviewers were members of the health care profession, they were naturally "right" and thus her feelings must be wrong.

3. With Regard to Therapist Self-Disclosure

We have reached the inevitable conclusion that therapists often pay lip service to the need for self-disclosure but do not actually do it. For example, at a recent presentation by a well-known and highly respected therapist, what was communicated to the audience was that therapist self-disclosure ought to always be carefully considered and never step beyond the parameters of statements such as "yes, I can relate to having a teen-age son go off to university."

In our view, this therapist's "self"-statement was a non-self-disclosing statement in that there was neither affect nor self-revelation involved. This therapist's assertion was that if one were to step beyond these boundaries of disclosure, one would lose one's credibility with the client. In our experience, as described below, it is precisely through this willingness on the therapist's part to truly self-disclose that he or she acquires a genuine credibility within the therapeutic relationship. Another therapeutic technique is the disclosure of a long-resolved emotional incident rather than a current grappling with those developmental growth crises which all of us are heir to over time.

These fraudulent self-disclosures create the illusion that the therapist "has it all together," and therefore perpetuate a relationship which is based on a lack of integrity. From the Integrity perspective, this in turn dramatically minimizes the therapist's potential effectiveness because only a relationship which is based explicitly on integrity will lead to lasting therapeutic improvement. This in turn implies a qualitative shift in the power distribution between therapist and patient, as one can only credibly challenge the behavior of another from the position of an equal. In this regard, Mowrer's phrase, now popularized in the self-help movements is apropos—"you can only talk the talk if you have walked the walk."

The principle of the effectiveness of self-disclosure and peer counseling has been well documented in the Alcoholics Anonymous movement. This nuance can have a profound impact on helper/helpee effectiveness. This is exemplified by the experience of the (second) author, in her 15-year career as a therapist, originally trained in the feeling-oriented therapies, but over recent years moving increasingly to an Integrity Therapy approach. At first, the prospect of sharing her own foibles and fraudulent past and present struggles with her clients was terrifying. Not only did this seem to violate every "rule in the book," but also she was terrified to show her own humanity, lest it challenge her credibility in the eyes of her client. In other words, she had bought into the double standard which is perpetuated by the mental health profession: While the client is encouraged to disclose all of the nitty-gritty details, the therapist is somehow to continue to present the facade of at least partial imperturbability to life's existential challenges. However, as she continued to struggle toward increased integrity in her own life, this double standard began to present her with an untenable sense of betrayal of herself, her clients, and the therapeutic relationship. After some practice, she has gotten over the "narcissistic injury" that her clients seemed relatively unaffected by her "dramatic" disclosures, and has found a dramatic shift in her sense of authenticity in the therapeutic relationship, in her effectiveness in truly challenging another, and in her overall therapeutic effectiveness, especially in her work with incest survivors who are particularly vulnerable to the potential sense of violation in a relationship. It is now her experiential and visceral awareness that it is fundamentally and qualitatively different to challenge her client when she herself has been psychologically naked and vulnerable, has shared not only past difficulties but also present turmoil, and has made an explicit contract with the patient that she (the therapist) herself will make herself as open to challenge on her own integrity within the therapeutic relationship as will the client! And, as a footnote, she discovered to her dismay as a further narcissistic injury that her clients had been the wiser anyway. One female client whom she had worked with in the past, and who returned to therapy, at which time the therapist shared some things about herself which she had never disclosed before, stated, "I didn't think that you had reached this understanding of life by just reading books!"

BETRAYAL AND VALUE CLASHES
WITHIN THE THERAPEUTIC RELATIONSHIP

As mental health professionals, we are all bound by the necessity to conform to professional standards of ethical conduct, but there is no single professional standard which addresses the issue of our underlying values as therapists. The unspoken implication that such a value choice does not exist can only be an illusory one, as in fact, value judgments must consistently and continually be made by the therapist at every moment within the therapeutic encounter. Psychotherapy training programs seldom isolate or focus on the question of the fit between the trainee's personal value system and the value assumptions underlying various theoretical models. It may be precisely in response to this paucity of "valuing" of value questions and dilemmas for the therapist that we have found an intense welcomed relief in our Value and Burn-out Workshops when mental health professionals are given an opportunity to explore these issues.

The concept of the therapist as a valuing animal has emerged as a useful means of reframing and elucidating the therapeutic impasse, avoiding the betrayal of the patient through the use of psychopathological jargon and psychiatric labelling of the client as an avoidance of therapist involvement and accountability in the interaction. The following vignettes, drawn from our therapeutic work, are offered to illustrate the manner in which resistance in the therapeutic process can be reformulated as stemming not from psychodynamic conflict but rather from a basic clash of values between therapist and client.

> 1. Tom, a 38-year-old male diagnosed as having a severe anxiety disorder, consistently "resisted" the therapist's confrontation of the lack of industry in his life. This impasse became reformulated once the discrepancy between Tom's strong belief that he should be entitled to live without having to "slug away 8 hours a day" and what he perceived as the therapist's strong "Protestant work ethic" was clarified.
> 2. Lisa, a 35-year-old woman diagnosed as having a "borderline personality disorder/rule out narcissistic" had incorporated the pop psychology concept that "self comes first," and

in fact had made a large poster stating "You're Number 1" to put up in her kitchen. The therapist came to realize that in her own rejection of this value she stood in opposition not only to her client but also to her mainstream professional colleagues. Sharing this difference in value with her client allowed a more open and genuine dialogue exchange to occur between them, which in turn allowed the client to gain a meaningful insight into some of the obstacles which were impeding her struggle toward becoming real.

To have adopted a more traditional interpretative or dynamic explanation in the above conflictual situations would have resulted in "missing the boat" through a devaluation and betrayal of the other by a psychopathological explanation framing the difficulty as a function of the other's pathology, rather than addressing the actual core conflictual issue. In both our own work and in vignettes shared by participants in our value workshops, the following clinical issues vis-à-vis the role of the therapist have arisen: the therapist's neutrality, his or her self-disclosure, confidentiality, physical contact with the patient, religious beliefs, personal moral code versus moral expectations of the others, perspectives on acting-out, feelings toward intense affect from others, and, finally, the therapist's functioning as a therapist at times when he or she is undergoing a personal crisis. A practical and poignant issue which seems to consistently crop up is that of how to handle an angry silence in a therapy session. In this regard, our colleagues are eager to explore a conflict between what they feel they have to do–namely to take the traditional therapeutic approach of (angrily) outwaiting the patient, and what they truly feel driven to do–namely, to speak up or encourage the patient to move away from the silent and withdrawn position. The issue of a clash between the therapist's own value system and the necessary adherence and allegiance to a given therapeutic framework has in fact emerged as a consistent and pivotal dilemma of valuing for many of the therapists with whom we have dialogued.

TRAINING ISSUES

The above experiences with both clients and colleagues have further led us to the belief that there is a vital and unmet need within the therapeutic training process to look at the role of the therapists' values within the therapeutic encounter. Neophyte therapists' awareness of self as a valuing animal would appear to be a critical and necessary condition in order for them to begin to freely risk discovering themselves as a therapeutic medium. The recognition of their own value system has then to be followed by the willingness to dare being accountable for how this works within the therapeutic relationship. While it may be difficult to find a perfect fit between the supervisor and supervisee's value systems, it would seem to behoove a training supervisor to be aware of the role that values may play within the supervisory relationship. Much as in a therapeutic relationship, the supervisor must become sensitive to the values of the supervisee, whereby there can be a mutual valuing of divergent perspectives, coming in essence to agree to disagree. Otherwise, this can be the beginning of a process of betrayal of the neophyte therapist by the "system," which will ultimately lead to a betrayal of both self and future therapeutic relationships with others. Also, as in the context of the therapeutic relationship, the resolution phase of a clash in values can occur as one comes to appreciate that only through a commitment to one's own value system can one allow for the presence of a divergent value system in the other. Only through this process can the concept of individual autonomy really begin to blossom. If on the other hand, if one (as supervisor, supervisee, therapist, or client) comes to violate one's own value system in order to preserve a given relationship, one is then in violation of one's own integrity, and therefore is in a betrayal of self, the other, and the relationship. This position is an open challenge to the popular view that the client is cured if he or she comes to share the value system of the therapist. For us, the latter view presents a moral dilemma, as we feel that a pivotal life task for every individual is that of discovering one's real self, which in one sense becomes the discovery of what one values, accompanied by the integrity to be true to this personal value system.

In the process of resolution of a clash in values, be it in a supervisory relationship or in a therapeutic relationship, we have found the Integrity Therapy model to provide a useful conceptual framework. Mowrer's metaphor of integrity as a three-legged stool based upon the elements of honesty, responsibility, and increased emotional closure with others, appears to offer a useful paradigm for a positive and healthy process of individuation focusing on the valuing of self and the valuing of others.

CONCLUSIONS

In conclusion, we feel that the therapeutic relationship may unwittingly betray the patient/client through a tendency to view the client's psychopathology solely as a function of the client's input into the therapeutic equation versus a consideration of the therapist's accountability within the therapeutic relationship. If, as therapists, we wish to be effective in helping our patients deal with the pain of betrayal outside of the therapeutic relationship, then perhaps we are beholden to becoming sensitive to the nuances inherent in psychotherapeutic ideologies which may create another and perhaps more insidious phenomenon of the *betrayed patient*, this time within the therapeutic relationship.

REFERENCES

Alexander, F. (1946). *Fundamentals of Psychoanalysis, 1st Ed.* New York: W. W. Norton.

Lander, N.R., & Nahon, D. (1986). *Treating the "untreatable" patient: A case study in unlabelling.* Paper presented at the American Psychological Association Annual Meeting, Washington, DC.

Lander, N.R., & Nahon, D. (1988). *Integrity therapy: A vision for the nineties.* Paper Presented at the XXIVth International Congress of Psychology, Sydney, Australia.

Lander, N.R., & Nahon, D. (1990). *Values of the therapist: The hidden dimension.* Paper Presented at the 22nd International Congress of Applied Psychology, Kyoto, Japan.

Mowrer, O.H. (1938). New evidence concerning the nature of psychopathology. *Studies in Psychotherapy and Behavior Change, 1,* 115-193.

Mowrer, O.H. (1953). Freedom and responsibility: A psychological analysis. *Journal of Legal Education, 6,* 60-78.

Mowrer, O.H. (1953). *Psychotherapy: Theory and research.* New York: The Ronald Press.

Mowrer, O.H. (1961). *The crisis in psychiatry and religion.* Princeton, NJ: D. Van Nostrand.

Mowrer, O.H. (1961). The rediscovery of responsibility. *Special Supplement on Psychiatry in American Life, Atlantic Monthly, 7,* 88-91.

Mowrer, O.H. (1964). *The new group therapy.* Princeton, NJ: D. Van Nostrand.

Mowrer, O.H. (1964). Freudianism, behaviour therapy and "self-disclosure." *Behavior Research & Therapy, 1,* 321-337.

Mowrer, O.H. (Ed.) (1967). *Morality and mental health.* Chicago: Rand McNally.

Mowrer, O.H. (1969). Too little and too late. *International Journal of Psychiatry, 7,* 536-556.

Mowrer, O.H. (1970). *The behavioural vs. disease model of psychopathology. Proceedings of the third annual meeting of the Association for the Advancement of Behavior Therapy.* New York: Academic Press.

Betrayal of the Feminine:
A Male Perspective

David N. Elkins

SUMMARY. At the societal level the "betrayal of the feminine" enthrones masculine biases and maintains the power structures of patriarchal societies. At the personal level a man who betrays the feminine side of himself cuts himself off from his soul and erodes his humanity and psychological health. Writing in autobiographical style, the author traces his own journey as a man toward acknowledging and integrating the feminine into his life. The "betrayal of the feminine" has important implications for our work with the psychotherapy patient.

This paper is about the betrayal of the feminine. I have come to believe that this betrayal permeates almost every aspect of our society including our philosophy, science, theology, epistemology, interpersonal relations; our views of morality; our treatment of the planet; and even our understanding of personality, psychopathology, and psychotherapy (see Belenky, Clinchy, Goldberger, and Tarule, 1986; Capra, 1982; Eisler, 1987; Faludi, 1991; Gilligan, 1982; Murdock, 1990; Stone, 1976.

At the personal level the betrayal of the feminine is equally

---

David N. Elkins, PhD, is Associate Professor of psychology in the Graduate School of Education and Psychology of Pepperdine University. He is a member of the executive boards of both the Association for Humanistic Psychology (AHP) and Division 32, Humanistic Psychology, of APA. He is also a member of the board of editors for the *Journal of Humanistic Psychology* and *The Psychotherapy Patient*. He maintains a private practice in Tustin, California, and is currently writing a book on psychotherapy, spirituality, and the art of nurturing the soul. Mailing address: Pepperdine University, Graduate School of Education and Psychology 400 Corporate Pointe Culver City, CA 90230.

insidious and destructive. Men who deny the feminine side of themselves diminish their souls and fail to touch the richness of life. My own struggle to acknowledge, understand, and integrate the feminine into my life as a man has been the central task of my life. Nothing else has so profoundly affected my growth as a person and as a therapist. Nothing else has so deeply influenced my sense of identity, my intimate relationships, my clinical work, my graduate teaching, and my general "way of being" in the world.

I have chosen to write this paper in autobiographical style and from a more "feminine" way of knowing. I could have written more impersonally, in "masculine" fashion, taking a sequential, tightly organized, left-brain swath through the richness of the topic. Instead, I wanted to write personally and put words on that which I have learned from my own experiences in life.

In contrast to my scientific training, which gave me an epistemological bias toward research as the road to all truth, I have come to believe that the laboratory of one's own soul and life experience, along with the personal, reflective knowledge that emerges from that laboratory, is the most powerful and useful form of knowledge we have, particularly in the human sphere. Not only is this realm the wellspring of literature, music, poetry, and art; it is also, I believe, the source of our deepest knowing and best work in psychotherapy.

In *Women's Ways of Knowing,* Belenky, Clinchy, Goldberger, and Tarule (1986) charge that masculine bias permeates our epistemology and that there are other, more personal and feminine ways of knowing. I believe they are correct and have come, in fact, to suspect that all knowledge is embedded in the personal context of the knower and that "objective knowledge" is a contradiction of terms. The separation of the knower from that which is known, so idealized in many scientific circles, may be only an epistemological myth that disguises the involvement we have with our knowledge.

Thus, I will not ask readers, as is usually done, to forgive the personal nature of this paper. Rather, I would hope that you might even embrace it as an alternative and more feminine way of basing and communicating knowledge. It is my hope that my personal, concrete story might touch more universal chords, speaking to the heart as well as to the head.

DEFINITION OF FEMININE

Following the lead of Carol Gilligan (1982) and Riane Eisler (1987),I am using the term "feminine" to refer to the softer, gentler side of ourselves, the side that emphasizes intimacy, nurturance, care, affiliation, relationship, intuition, personalness, peacefulness, creativity, and working *with* nature and with others. Thus, the feminine refers to that constellation of human qualities which are often the polar opposite of such "masculine" emphases as distance, control, separation, rationality, analytical thinking, hierarchical positioning, competing, mastering, conquering, having "power over," using force or violence to resolve conflict, valuing principle over person, and working against nature and others to subdue them.

The terms feminine and masculine are clearly problematic, since they seem to imply that certain qualities are gender specific and that women cannot have the masculine qualities and men cannot have the feminine qualities. But I believe these terms, once this is understood, still communicate better than others that have been suggested. And I hope this paper will demonstrate that these qualities need not be gender specific but that men can,and in fact must, develop and integrate the feminine qualities into their lives.

MY MOTHER: INITIATION INTO THE FEMININE

My mother died October 20, 1990, and in the deep reflections associated with her death I once again realized how important she had been in shaping my basic character and in giving me a fundamental appreciation of the "feminine" side of my personality.

Mom had an eighth-grade education and, except for a brief period in Kansas City when she was very small, she lived out her entire life in the foothills of the Ozark Mountains in northeastern Arkansas. She was not a feminist nor even a "strong woman" by today's criteria. But she was a woman who loved her three children and whose highest joy was to nurture them. When we were little, she breast-fed us, rocked us, sang to us, laid us on her ample body, hugged us, said she loved us, told us bedtime stories, listened to our problems and dreams, defended us, and comforted us when we were sick or in pain. When I was a young boy she introduced me to her women friends and took me to various gatherings of women. I can remember how kind the women were to me and how they nurtured me with attention and care. From these experiences I learned how wonderful women can be, and I think I fell in love with women and the feminine very early in life. From Mom's example and love I learned the meaning of nurturance, empathy, kindness, care, and truly "being there" for another. I feel she imprinted my soul with the feminine and awakened that side of me so profoundly that I could never shut it off no matter how hard I tried in life. And I did try, as the following will show.

THE OEDIPAL PERIOD:
FIRST BETRAYAL OF THE FEMININE?

In rural Arkansas, where I grew up, "boys were boys" and "girls were girls," and there were clear expectations about each gender's dress, activities, interests, attitudes, and hair length. Although my mother had effectively initiated me into the feminine, at an early age I began a concerted effort to deny that side of myself and to fit the masculine stereotype expected of a young boy growing up in that milieu. I developed an interest in hunting and fishing, became a good shot with a rifle, played baseball and basketball, had a boyish, masculine body, and, to my memory, was never called a "sissy"–the most feared and insulting taunt of boyhood!

This denial of the feminine and identification with the masculine began about the time of oedipal resolution. While Freud would have been proud of me, I have wondered if the oedipal conflict and its ideal resolution according to classical theory is not rather the first "betrayal of the feminine" for a male child growing up in a patriarchal society. I wonder how these oedipal dynamics would differ between a boy and his parents in a matriarchal or partnership society where feminine traits were as highly valued as masculine. In such a society would it still be dynamically necessary or culturally expected that a young boy make such a decisive break from the feminine and establish such a strong identification with the masculine? Or is it possible that in a society where gender boundaries and expectations were not so rigid that little boys would maintain stronger identity connections with the mother while at the same time affirming their gender identification with the father? Carol Gilligan (1982) said that girls establish their identity through affiliation with the same-gender mother, while boys, being of the opposite gender from the mother, must establish their identity by separation. Thus, Gilligan believes that little girls grow up to fear individuation, which threatens their identity founded on affiliation, while little boys grow up to fear intimacy, which threatens their identity based on separation. In general, I believe Gilligan is correct and that most of us go through the process of identity formation she describes, as well as the classical oedipal conflict and resolution described by Freud. But are these dynamics and processes the expression of some biological or gender-based inevitability, or are they rather an early manifestation of a patriarchal society's interest in grooming young boys to betray the feminine and to identify with those masculine traits which will eventually allow them to take their "rightful" place in the masculine power structures? Is the oedipal conflict and resolution a healthy process of identity formation for the young boy, or is it a pathological betrayal of the feminine, of that which makes him most deeply human? These are not intended to be rhetorical questions, but they are intended to challenge a central theoretical tenet of classical theory which seems, as so much psychological theory does, to justify the exaltation of the masculine and the repression of the feminine.

Today, I often see young men who were raised in families where gender boundaries and stereotypes were not so rigid. These young men, including my two sons, are clearly different. I am deeply touched by their ability to openly acknowledge and express their more feminine qualities. Sometimes I feel a nostalgic sadness for my own childhood and wish I could have known that kind of openness in myself, my brother, my father, and the other boys and men I grew up with. It seems such an unnecessary loss and waste. How I long in retrospect for a father who could have broken through his own barriers and hugged me, nurtured me, cried with me, and told me with feeling, "I love you so much!" Even as a man of 47 I still long for that, and this is one reason the "betrayal of the feminine" is such a tragedy for us men. Such betrayal of the gentler side of ourselves leaves us emotionally mute and prevents us from giving one another the masculine nurturance we all need as little boys and even as grown men. This betrayal creates tragic chasms between ourselves as males: between fathers and sons, brother and brother, friend and friend, man and man.

PUBERTY AND DEPRESSION

In the summer of 1958, when I was 13, I became depressed. I would lie on my bed through those hot Arkansas days, an electric fan blowing over my body, and ruminate about my life. I felt sad, lost, scared, and very much alone in the world. Many years later a Jungian analyst would call that depression my "calling." And so it was. At the time it certainly did not feel like anything so noble, but I now understand what he meant. The depression was a call to know my soul more deeply.

In retrospect I believe the etiological root of that depression was the betrayal and loss of the feminine in my life. Like most boys, because of my need to be accepted as masculine, I had denied the feminine in myself. Of course, at 13, as I stood on the threshold of adolescence, this denial became even more pronounced. And like so many other women, my mother, who was a wonderful nurturer of the young child, was not quite sure what to do with me at puberty with my emerging sexuality as a young man. While she could confirm my feminine attributes such as kindness and love, she found it extremely difficult even to acknowledge, much less confirm, my masculine sexuality. Due, no doubt, to her discomfort, she withdrew from me, taking with her the nurturance I so desperately needed and failing to confirm my emerging sexuality as a young man.

Last year, in the week following her death, I stood alone at my mother's grave, thinking of the wonderful things she had given me but also aware of the gaping hole she had left by this failure to confirm my sensuality and sexuality as a man. I am convinced that mothers, who so often provide the feminine foundations for their sons, must also confirm their emerging sexuality and masculinity Just as fathers need to confirm the feminine as well as the masculine sides of their sons, mothers must also confirm both sides. Otherwise, the feminine and masculine may remain separated, unintegrated in a man, causing him to swing in polarity fashion from the masculine in some situations to the feminine in others, but never quite knowing how to be both masculine and feminine at the same time.

Women often speak of the sadness and confusion they felt at puberty when their fathers, uncomfortable with their daughter's developing body and sexuality, pulled away and stopped touching and nurturing them. Although they may tend to deny it more, I believe boys experience the same pain if their mothers withdraw from them at puberty. In fact, the loss may be even more intense for boys, since in many families the mother is the primary, and sometimes only, source of nurturance they have. I know that my experience was that I felt very alone and needed to be loved and nurtured, even while denying this. Being religious, in my loneliness I turned to God for help; but he was male and offered only rules, commands, threats, and judgments. Like the other males in my life, he did not know how to nurture my soul.

Rites of Passage

In this connection, I would like to discuss "rites of passage" and the need for rituals to assist young men from childhood to adulthood. I have listened to Joseph Campbell (Moyers & Tatge, 1988) and others tell of primitive tribes whose rituals make it unmistakably clear when a boy becomes a man. Longing for such clarity in my own life, I once viewed these primitive rituals with romantic, Rousseau-like innocence, seeing them as expressions of a natural order that our more complex society had lost.

But there is something about such primitive rituals, imposed by patriarchal men, which increasingly bothers me. Typically, the ritual involves adult males taking the boys into a secret place and putting them through a frightening, painful initiation. A boy is deemed to have become a man when he has endured all the initiation trials without showing fear or pain. The initiates are then instructed as to how they must treat, or *mistreat* would be more accurate, the females in the tribe. This often involves such "manly" things as rejecting former female playmates, not speaking to females, or only giving orders to them, including the boy's own mother, as though manhood is somehow synonymous with subjugation of women. I now see such "natural" rites of passage as being heavily contaminated by patriarchal attitudes and values designed to ensure that young men will deny the feminine in themselves and identify with a tribal system founded on male power and dominance over women. Subjugation of women is no more attractive among primitives than it is among Ivy League graduates.

But this is not to deny the need for rites of passage. Our society presents such confusing images that most young men are never quite sure what marks their passage to manhood, whether it is their Bar Mitzvah, their confirmation, their first sexual experience, getting drunk, joining a club, joining a gang, joining the army, turning 18, turning 21, being taken to a prostitute by an uncle or peer, getting married, having a child, becoming a grandfather, or retiring!

Since our society provides no clear demarcation for this passage, I think it could be very meaningful if a boy's family created a private ritual to recognize this important passage in his life. It seems to me that such a ritual should confirm both his masculine power and his feminine gentleness. This would be an opportune time for a mother to confirm her son's masculinity and need for power and strength, and a time for his father to show him that manhood involves gentleness and care. I suspect a boy would never forget such a ritual and that it would provide him with an indelible definition and map of manhood.

Men and Masculinity

It is somewhat ironic that in our patriarchal society, which encourages males to betray the feminine, men are equally unsure about their masculinity. As various books and "gatherings of men" attest, many men are now seeking to reclaim their masculinity. I feel in deep accord with these men; and while this article is about the betrayal of the feminine in men, I believe it is also about the recovery of our masculinity. A major part of a man's journey to reclaiming his masculinity is the acceptance of his feminine side. Every woman of depth knows that the feminine is a major part of a man's masculine appeal. Men also recognize the importance of this dimension in their workshops and friendships when they cease competing and reach out in gentle caring to one another. As the truly feminine woman is one who has moved beyond effeminacy to her deepest power and strength, so a truly masculine man is one who has moved beyond "machismo" to the gentlest regions of his soul. A whole person, whether woman or man, is one whose feminine and masculine sides have intertwined themselves in mutual respect and support for each other.

BECOMING A MINISTER: THE FEMININE AND MASCULINE IN RELIGION

While my depression at 13 made me more introspective, I think I missed its deeper message. I continued to deny the feminine in my life and to emphasize my adolescent masculinity. But the feminine, no matter how repressed or purged, has a way of reasserting itself. Like a "faithful remnant" of the soul, it remains true even when we are not and finds ways to reenter our lives. In my own case, I was deeply drawn to writing, poetry, and romantic feelings. And although my religion was dominated by a male God and male values, I nevertheless sensed the feminine possibilities in its emphasis on love, kindness, and service and was deeply drawn to the mystery and numinosity of my religious tradition. At an early age I dreamed of two vocations–being a writer or being a minister. I now have no doubt that these stirrings were signs that my feminine side– betrayed, dammed up, and prevented from direct expression–was nevertheless cutting new channels for itself in my life.

As time went on, religion increasingly became the center of my life. In the rural communities of Arkansas religion was important and the culturally sanctioned way for people to feed their souls. I went to church regularly and was deeply moved by the rituals of my religion. For me, the real value of these rituals was their inner appeal, the intrinsic aspects that fed my soul. Prayer became a way of centering my soul and gaining a transformative perspective on my life. Religious songs would often move me to tears. Poignant sermons would touch and heal my heart. And the ritual of baptism, which my church emphasized strongly, with its symbolism of death, burial, and resurrection, touched an archetypal dimension in my soul. Also, in that rather austere culture my church was almost the only place I could hear adults talk about love. When I decided to study for the ministry, I am sure I saw in that vocation an opportunity to be respected as a man (ministers are respected in rural Arkansas!) and at the same time express my feminine side in a culturally approved way.

But it would be a mistake for me to leave the impression that my religion was somehow a haven for the feminine. While it had a dimension of softness and gentleness, it was highly masculinized in most of its theology and outward forms. God was definitely male, and the public worship was conducted entirely by men. Women were required to keep silent in the public assembly lest they "usurp authority" over the men. Our very masculine "God the Father" was exacting, demanding, judgmental, intolerant, and punitive. If one wanted God's love and grace, one had to "toe the line" and do nothing to anger or displease him. Above all, one must be "right," theologically and morally. In one's personal life, one had continually to be on guard lest one's words, actions, or thoughts might become tinged with sin. In short, in order to enjoy God's acceptance and love, one had to endure the hell of his wrath and exacting demands. This was the male God who lived in the village churches of northeastern Arkansas and the only God I had ever known. At the time this male God did not seem strange or pathological at all; in fact he seemed very much like most of the men I knew.

But in college I had some wonderful theology professors who taught me about the feminine side of Christianity. They talked of love, grace, and a gentle God revealed through the feminine qualities of Jesus. I was very drawn to this new image of God, and gradually my theology became more "feminized." As a young ministerial student speaking in country churches, I began to emphasize love, caring, grace, tolerance, kindness, and serving others. While most parishioners seemed to enjoy these sermons, others seemed to feel I was "going soft" and encouraged me to talk more about the demands and judgments of God. I found this increasingly hard to do. I needed a more feminine God who would love, nurture, and accept me as I was; I assumed most of my parishioners needed the same.

Sara and I were married in 1963. After graduating from college, I became the minister of a church in Michigan where I became friends with two ministers of my denomination whose theological training had taken them beyond the narrow boundaries of our conservative church. Both men were warm and nurturing, and I was very drawn to them. They became my spiritual mentors, and I began to grow–which was the wrong thing for a minister of a conservative church to do in the 1960s.

The 1960s was a decade of great change and friction in America between "the establishment" and the younger generation. I clearly identified with the younger generation and felt increasingly frustrated by the rigidity and intolerance of my church. In those days many churches joined together to help address the pressing social issues of that period. My church would have nothing to do with any of this, remaining separate, isolated, and uninvolved. Eventually, my two minister friends got into conflict with the leadership of their congregations. They were branded as "dangerous liberals" and were fired and then excommunicated. When I defended them, the leaders in my congregations also fired and excommunicated me. Although this was a devastating blow to my future in the church, I never felt depressed or even deeply discouraged. Intuitively, I knew life was carrying me in the right direction.

Male Gods and Patriarchal Religions

Kierkegaard said we live life forwards and understand it backwards. As I look back at my church and my untimely demise as a minister, I now see the betrayal of the feminine at the heart of those dynamics. As Eisler (1987) has so powerfully pointed out, it is very difficult for a male God, and those who follow him, to tolerate too much of the feminine. As ancient patriarchal gods subjugated the goddesses, so modern religious men, also threatened by the feminine, will respond with hurt and violence if the threat becomes too great. As my own experience confirmed, even male ministers will be punished if they confront patriarchal attitudes and take feminine values too seriously.

And women hardly have a chance in patriarchal religion. The sexism that pervades conservative religion would result in multimillion-dollar lawsuits in any other societal institution. The theology of most conservative churches is blatantly sexist, and the submission of women to men is praised as godliness. Single and divorced women are second-class citizens; working mothers are made to feel guilty; little girls are taught in Sunday School to submit to God first and their husbands second. And all this violence to the female spirit is sanctioned by a patriarchal theology that disguises it as "the will of God."

I believe in God, but I cannot believe in that one any more. I cannot believe in a God who crushes the spirit of little girls and grooms little boys to become bigots. I cannot believe in a God who tells women they must bow in submission to a man. I cannot believe in a God who condemns assertive women but confirms violent men. I cannot believe in a God, so threatened in his own masculinity, that he cannot even hear the voice of the feminine if it dares question his authority. This God is too old and too savage for those who long for a "partnership" society in which women and men respect each other as equals and rejoice in the dignity, strength, and differences of the other.

JUNGIAN THERAPY AND THE ANIMA: RAPPROCHEMENT WITH THE FEMININE

In 1976 I was in my predoctoral internship, trying to write my dissertation, struggling in my marriage, and feeling generally overwhelmed and depressed. I decided to enter therapy and did so with a Jungian analyst. He was 73 years of age and had received much of his analytical training at Jung's Institute in Zurich. Since I was a financially destitute graduate student, he agreed to see me for a reduced fee.

Thus began the most healingful journey of my life. At the end of my first session, after listening carefully to the half-articulate longings of my heart, he said simply, "You are spiritually hungry." I knew he was profoundly correct. By this time I had left the ministry, dedicated myself to doctoral work, and completely lost contact with my feminine side. My soul was hungry for spiritual nurturance, and my depression was once again the direct result of my betrayal of the feminine, my failure to nurture my soul.

The Anima Archetype

The first dream I brought to therapy was of a beautiful woman, dressed in a flowing white dress, dancing by herself. She moved and twirled slowly and gracefully, lost in her own mysteries, parts of her dress catching and floating on the breeze as she danced. She was a numinous figure and an archetypal woman. Between me and her was a thick glass wall. I could see her clearly through the glass, but I could not talk to her, touch her, nor dance with her. The glass wall separated us; I was on my side of the wall; she was on hers.

"That," my Jungian analyst said, "is your anima." While I had read a little Jungian theory, I really had no idea what he meant. As I was to learn, he meant that the woman in the dream was my feminine side. In the dream I was entranced and drawn to her, but we were separated by the glass wall. Thus, the therapeutic task, which extended over many months, was to help me remove the wall, to come to know my anima or feminine side more deeply, to touch, twirl, and dance with her in my life. (I realize that to those unfamiliar with Jungian theory, my way of describing my therapy may sound very strange. But if you have read this far, perhaps you are gradually becoming desensitized to strangeness and can bear a little more!)

Anima Projections and Therapeutic Growth

My therapy was greatly facilitated by the fact that for five years I had had a close female friend who in many ways was the embodiment of my anima archetype; or, as the Jungians would say, she at least resembled my anima enough to constellate my anima projections. Interestingly, this woman was not my wife; and, in fact, one of the reasons I had entered therapy was that I was so drawn to this woman friend that I was not sure what this meant for my marriage. My relationship to this woman, while not a sexual affair, was certainly an affair of the soul. I felt as though I had always known her, and I seemed to find and know myself better in the intimacy of our friendship. Fortunately for me, I also had an accepting, caring wife whom I loved, and who loved me deeply. All my past cultural, religious, and parental training had told me it was impossible to love two women, at least at the same time. But my experience was that I deeply loved Sara, my wife; and I had also come to love this female friend, whose name is Dot.

Dot caught my anima projections, and as an externalization of my archetype, she provided an unusual opportunity for me to know this side of myself and to develop it more deeply. So for awhile Dot became the focus of my therapy. Encouraged by my analyst to deal with my "Dot side," as he called it, I talked about her, dreamed about her in various images, wrote letters never mailed to her, and even wrote poems to her. Through such Jungian therapeutic techniques, I gradually realized that the intense, sometimes romanticized feelings, thoughts, and dreams about Dot were really more about a lost feminine side of myself that was now emerging and struggling to be born. As this realization dawned, Dot as a person became less central in my therapy, and what she represented in me became the focus. I saw that while Dot was a truly wonderful person in her own right, that which she had constellated in me was uniquely me and mine. I slowly began to "own back" those feelings, stirrings, and qualities I had attributed to and projected onto her. I began to appreciate and actively affirm my feminine side and the increasing depth of experiencing that it brought into my life. Instead of feeling embarrassed about my gentleness, kindness, and empathic abilities and wondering, in typical male fashion, if these qualities somehow made me less a man, I began to embrace these neglected parts of my soul and to integrate them into my masculinity.

As my therapy progressed, I came to feel for the first time that I knew who I was, that I was touching something of my fundamental identity. I think that is what happens when one shifts toward the soul. Living from this more centered place, I felt more confident, more quietly sure of myself. Life took on depth and passion. My depression completely lifted, and I had never felt so healthy, so whole in my life. I would not go so far as to say that in this therapy I "came home" to my soul; but I would say that I finally learned where "home" was and how healing it felt to go there once in awhile.

When my therapy came to an end, my analyst gave me two pieces of advice. First, he recommended that I return to therapy about every 5 years as a way of "weeding my garden" and ensuring my continued growth. Second, he said I should always have female friends, women of depth, in my life. He felt their friendship would nurture my soul and help prevent me from becoming depressed. Unwaveringly supportive of Sara and my marriage throughout the therapy and always demanding that I take responsibility for my projections, he nevertheless recognized the very real value of female friends and the capacity of certain women to nurture a man's soul. His advice that I always have female friends has proven to be one of the wisest prescriptions I have ever received.

My analyst died in 1979, not long after my therapy ended, and sometimes I miss him very much. He was one of the few men I have known who could nurture the soul; and I will always remember him as the one who, in adulthood, introduced me to my anima and showed me the value of my feminine side. Sometimes I miss him very much and wish I could see him one more time to tell him how much his gentle, knowing guidance has meant to my life.

FEMALE FRIENDS: FOLLOWING MY ANALYST'S ADVICE

It has now been 14 years since my Jungian therapy ended and my therapist recommended I always have female friends. Next to Sara, my wife of 28 years, Dot is still my best friend, and our friendship has now survived and grown for 21 years. The three of us have a relationship now characterized by trust, caring, and an intimacy that feels like "family." (Both Sara and Dot read this manuscript before submission and gave me permission to include their names and the personal material related to them.)

Dot is a strong woman of depth and wisdom. She is a therapist who is acutely attuned to women and women's issues. She is kind, gentle, and unconditionally accepting. A few months ago she gave me a pledge of friendship that touched my heart. She told me, "As long as there is breath in my body, I will be your friend. And anything I have is yours. Just ask." I am deeply grateful that life has given me such a friend.

Sara is my most intimate friend, as well as my wife. She is a strong, warm, sensual woman who at midlife is growing in remarkable ways. An accountant who spent many years in her head, she is now moving into her body, her intuition, and her feminine depths. Strongly drawn to the feminine herself, Sara has intimate friendships with several women and is finding that others are looking to her as a mentor and model of a strong, feminine woman. I am deeply pleased that Sara chose, and continues to choose, to share her life with me. Her presence and being nurture my soul. In a way, this article is a tribute to both Sara and Dot and to that which they have awakened and nurtured in me for half my life.

Sometimes I feel sad for men who have no intimate friendships with women. Male friends can be wonderful and nothing here is meant to disparage the deep relationships men are sometimes able to forge with one another. Still, there is something unique about friendship with a woman; and there are some things about oneself, and life, and nurturance of the soul that a man can never learn until he has a female friend. To sit, late at night, on opposite ends of a sofa, sipping hot tea, with music in the background, a fireplace or oil lamp burning, and to speak one's soul to another–that is what life was meant to be.

My analyst was right. I will always need female friends. And, thank God, I have them.

MIDLIFE:
COMING HOME TO THE FEMININE FOR GOOD?

Like most men, I have betrayed the feminine again and again in my life. Each time, this betrayal has led eventually to emptiness or depression. When this became painful enough, I would be forced to pay attention to my feminine side and to seek out the nurturance my soul needed.

My most recent experience with this pattern was 4 years ago. I had become obsessed with certain ego pursuits connected with my job, and various midlife issues were coming to the fore. I was completely neglecting my soul and, once again, betraying my feminine side. As my history would have predicted, I slowly began to feel anxious and depressed. But this time the depression, which at other times had been mild and lasted only 2 or 3 months, was more severe and lasted almost a year. This scared me, and I felt my soul was giving me a midlife ultimatum, "Take care of me and nurture me, or else!"

And finally, after enough pain, I decided to take my feminine side seriously which, in spite of all my therapy, experience, and insights, I had never really done before. Like most therapists, I am a caretaker and find it easier to take care of others than to admit my own needs. But I am learning and have made some progress. For example, I have worked to open my soul more to Sara; I have contacted Dot on a more frequent basis; I have developed two new friendships with women; I have a new male friend; I am writing a book on spirituality; I have begun to write poetry and short stories; I have begun to dance; I listen to music (instead of talk shows!) on my car radio; I have bought a cabin in the mountains and go there regularly; I have begun to lead "growth groups" again; I have taken a course of massage treatments; I am more in contact with my body and my sensuality; I am in strong contact with my artistic and creative side; I have changed the way I teach my graduate psychology classes, integrating music, poetry and feminine ways of knowing into my teaching; I have begun to reach out more to my students and my clients, providing them with more nurturance and care; and I am spending more hours sitting at night with an intimate friend, sipping hot tea, with music in the background, a fireplace or oil lamp burning. . . .

Carl Jung once said that we either get a "self" at midlife or not at all. He also said he had never healed a midlife patient who had not recovered a spiritual orientation to "life. Finally, at 47 I think I know what he meant; and sometimes I even hope I might be coming home for good.

BETRAYAL OF THE FEMININE: IMPLICATIONS AND DISCUSSION

The betrayal of the feminine has important implications for our work with the psychotherapy patient. In this final section I would like to make some theoretical observations and discuss the relevance of this topic to clinical practice.

First, in this paper I have used the terms anima, soul, and feminine side somewhat interchangeably. While each term has its own etymology, connotations, and theoretical associations, I believe all three terms point to that same basic phenomenological constellation that in this article I am calling "the feminine." Since they are important constructs, I would like to say more about the anima and soul.

The Anima

The discovery of the anima by Carl Jung is a fascinating story. During his descent into his own unconscious, Jung heard a woman's voice speak to him. Intrigued by this part of himself, he talked with her in an effort to discover who she was. He stated, "My conclusion was that she must be the 'soul,' in the primitive sense, and I began to speculate on the reasons why the name 'anima' was given to the soul" (Jung, 1961, p. 186). Later, Jung came to believe that this anima or "woman within" is an archetype in the collective unconscious of men. (Since women are the embodiment of anima or soul, their corresponding archetype is the animus, which is masculine.) But the point I would like to emphasize is that Jung saw these two constructs, anima and soul, as pointing to the same internal reality. Thus, to speak of a man's "feminine side," as I do in this paper, is to speak of his anima or soul.

The Soul

Psychology once meant "the study of the soul." But more complex and desacralized constructs, models, and definitions soon replaced that simple formulation. Psychology is now dominated by medical and mechanistic models which leave little room for the soul. These models, which appeal to the scientific and technological mind set of many American therapists, show us how to eliminate depression or anxiety almost as easily as our family physician medicates a sore throat or our trained mechanic tunes our Ford or Mercedes. Personally, I find medical and mechanistic models extremely seductive. Like most psychologists, my training steeped me in the assumptions underlying these models, and a part of me would find it quite satisfying to be a "junior physician" or a "mechanic of the psyche." But a deeper, wiser part of me knows that these models desacralize the human being and obscure something fundamental about our nature. The word "soul" points to that which has been obscured; and the therapist as "healer of the soul" recovers the sacred dimension of therapy.

For me, soul is not an arbitrary construct but a word that points to a phenomenological reality of which I am aware in my subjective world. I know and can feel when I am in contact with, or am living from my soul. There are certain words which as inadequate as they are, do capture something of the feel of soul. Such words include centeredness, peacefulness, nonstriving, artistic, gentleness, flowing, a sense of depth, quiet joy, lovingness, heartfeltness, spiritual, earthiness, sensuality, meditative, being, passive action, feminine. I also know my soul by the familiar "feeling" of mood and affect I experience when my soul is being moved, stirred, and touched. Certain music, poetry, movies, plays, pieces of literature, and even cities and memories touch my soul, sometimes profoundly; and I can feel it stir within me, like a pregnant woman feeling her baby move in the night. And it is this poignant phenomenological "feel," much more than observation of my outward behavior, which tells me whether or not I am in contact with my soul, whether or not I am living soulfully in my life.

As a therapist, I can only be a "healer of the soul" when I am in contact with and reaching out from my own soul. Buber (1970) recognized this when he said that the I of the I-Thou relationship is very different from the I of the I-It relationship. Mechanistic models make an "It" of both me and my client; soulfulness makes a "Thou" of us both and creates a relationship where healing of the soul becomes possible. Of course, no therapist can or even should live in the world of I-Thou all the time; but as Buber says, "Without It a human being cannot live. But whoever lives only with that is not human" (p. 85).

Psychopathology and the Betrayal of the Feminine

In this paper I traced how my personal "betrayal of the feminine" diminished me as a male and produced pathology in my life.

When a man cuts himself off from his soul, he is then consigned to live only from his masculine ego. The ego is very different from the soul. It strives, competes, manipulates, orchestrates; and it is controlling, clutching, demanding, possessive, and aggressive. If serving the soul, a man's ego can be healthy and effective; but when cut off from the soul and serving its own self-aggrandizement, the ego will eventually drive a man into some form of pathology. In such cases, the reconnection with and nurturance of the soul is the key to psychological recovery.

In this formulation psychopathology becomes the cry of the soul for attention, and symptoms and signs are messages of pain from the client's deeper feminine nature. Obviously, pathology can be complex, and this simple formulation will not always be useful. But my experience has been that the vast majority of clients desperately need to have their souls nurtured and fed. I am coming more and more to believe that the heart of much psychopathology is the betrayal of the feminine within ourselves, the neglect and abuse of our souls.

Psychotherapy and Nurturing the Soul

I have also come to believe that psychotherapy at its best is nurturing and healing the soul.

Our profession is characterized by a great diversity of theoretical models and therapeutic techniques; yet healing takes place regardless of the therapist's orientation and treatment procedures. While theory and technique are clearly important, and some approaches are more useful than others for a particular disorder or patient, I am convinced that a more basic factor is at work in therapeutic healing. I believe that factor is the nurturance of the soul which occurs through the therapist's caring, empathy, and honesty. As Truax and Carkhuff (1967) pointed out over 20 years ago, such human variables often have more to do with therapeutic healing than the particular theory and treatment techniques of the therapist. As Burton (1974) said, "All therapeutic systems help, and they seem to do so by a phenomenological humanism which sneaks in the back door of the cognitively-oriented treatment" (p. 168).

Psychological research long ago established the fact that the quality of the therapist-patient relationship is a crucial factor in therapeutic healing (Barrett-Lennard, 1962; Bergin & Jasper, 1969; Rogers, 1975; Truax & Carkhuff, 1967). As Yalom (1980) points out, there are literally "hundreds of research studies" which support the conclusion that "a positive relationship between patient and therapist is positively related to therapy outcome" and that "the single most important lesson the psychotherapist must learn" is that "it is the relationship that heals" (p. 401).

But what is meant by "the relationship heals"? I believe that is another way of saying that the therapist nurtures the client's soul, and through this nurturance the client is healed. There is probably no greater human need, from infancy to old age, than to be loved. Scientists have known since the 1940s, and parents for millennia, that the infant who is not loved becomes psychologically damaged and may even physically die. But the need for love does not end with childhood; it remains a primary psychological need throughout life. In the therapeutic relationship love refers to such nurturing factors as empathy, kindness, caring, warmth, and acceptance of the client. These factors make soul-to-soul contact possible; and they heal because they awaken and nurture the client's soul.

While human relationships are, I believe, the major source of nurturance for the feminine, other experiences and activities can also feed the soul. Almost anything which touches, stirs, or speaks to our depths has this capacity. Literature, poetry, music, paintings, sculptures, plays, dance, religion, nature, the creative process in ourselves–all these are sources of nurturance for the soul. For many, the artistic experience, whether creating or appreciating art, is particularly nurturing. While the intensity of creating can exhaust, maim, or even slay the artist, the soul is never more alive than when burning itself up in the flames of creative passion. And experiencing Michelangelo's *David* or *Pietà* or listening to a symphony of Beethoven may be such rich food for the soul that there are no words, only tears, to express the reverence and gratitude felt. In such experiences "depth speaks to depth," as Paul Tillich would say, and our souls are restored.

But it is not only the classics that can heal the soul. I grew up in a rural culture where the classics were generally unknown, and I dislike an elitism that implies only classical art or music can feed the soul. Primitive peoples, cut off from our civilization and from all experience of the classics, nevertheless create indigenous ways to feed the soul. And in the mountains of Arkansas the country people sing at church, play their homemade instruments, dance their quaint dances, whittle and carve their creations, and, in their own way, cast their artistic heart cries onto the seas of time. And while the sophisticated may cringe, it is nevertheless true that a country song by Willie Nelson, or the rhythmic cadence of a black preacher's voice, or the impassioned rendition of "Amazing Grace" by a church choir may feed rural souls better than a symphony of Beethoven or a painting of Van Gogh ever could. "Soul food" is whatever feeds the soul; and if one wishes to nurture the soul, one must seek those experiences and activities, whatever their nature or level of sophistication, that truly meet the hunger of one's own unique soul.

Thus, in our work with clients, or in taking care of ourselves as therapists, we must discover that which nurtures and feeds the soul. In this model the psychotherapist is first and foremost a healer of the soul. And psychotherapy is both a relationship in which we nurture our clients as well as a quest to help them discover in life that which feeds and heals their souls.

CONCLUSION

In a patriarchal society it is not easy for a man to acknowledge and integrate the feminine side of himself. Beginning in childhood, he is taught to exalt the masculine and to betray the feminine. But a man who denies or fails to develop his feminine side will have great difficulty nurturing the soul of another, whether wife, child, friend, or client. He will also have great difficulty with himself. Unable to nurture his own soul, he will know an unnamed emptiness, which he may try to fill with money, prestige, power, superficial sexual affairs, or other ego pursuits. It is not easy for a mane to recognize "soul hunger" in himself and to move from the stressful, competitive strivings of the masculine ego to the accepting, gentle feminine peacefulness of the soul. But this, it seems to me, is the journey each man must make if he wishes to find himself and drink deeply of life. And to make this journey, he must learn how to nurture, and allow others to nurture his feminine side, his soul. The soul is the center of our being, and the source of our identity. A man who learns to live from his soul, to live soulfully, will know the depth, passion, and intensity of existence. In coming home to his feminine side, he will find himself in consonance with the deeper, spiritual mysteries and rhythms of life. The key to real living is the recovery and nurturance of the soul.

REFERENCES

Barrett-Lennard, G. (1962). Dimensions of therapist response as causal factors in therapeutic change. *Psychological Monographs* 76, 43 (whole no. 562).

Belenky, M.F., Clinchy, B.M., Goldberger, N.R., & Tarule, J.M. (1986). *Women's ways of knowing.* New York: Basic Books.

Bergin, A., & Jasper, L. (1969). Correlates of empathy in psychotherapy: A replication. *Journal of Abnormal Psychology,* 174:477-81.

Buber, M. (1970). *I and thou.* New York: Charles Scribner's Sons.

Burton, A. (Ed.). (1976). *Operational theories of personality.* New York: Brunner/ Mazel.

Capra, F. (1982). *The turning point: Science, society, and the rising culture.* New York: Simon and Schuster.

Eisler, R. (1987). *The chalice and the blade.* San Francisco: Harper & Row.

Faludi, S. (1991). *Backlash: The undeclared war against American women.* New York: Crown Publishers.

Gilligan, C. (1982). *In a different voice: Psychological theory and women's development.* Cambridge: Harvard University Press.

Jung, C. (1961). *Memories, dreams, and reflections.* New York: Pantheon.

Moyers, B. (Executive Editor), & Tatge, C. (Producer). (1980). *'Joseph Campbell and the power of myth.* Videotape. New York: Mystic Fire Video, Inc.

Murdock, M. (1990). *The heroine's journey.* Boston: Shambhala.

Stone, M. (1976). *When God was a woman.* New York: Harcourt Brace Jovanovich.

Truax, C., & Carkhuff, R. (1967). *Toward effective counseling and psychotherapy: Training and practice.* Chicago: Aldine.

Yalom, I. (1980). *Existential psychotherapy.* New York: Basic Books.

Summoning Up the Murderer:
Betrayal of the Betrayed

E. Mark Stern

SUMMARY. The third-born of a family deeply wounded by the disappearance/murder of their first-born undertakes psychotherapy for his obsessive acting-out of masochistic fantasies.

He was dubbed "Teddy." There was a mysterious quality to his narrative as if he had lost his way in the undergrowth of fitful and disconnected chatter. At 23, the experience of a unitary self was blockaded by tenacious emotional oscillations. Teddy was betrayed by his fascination with the grotesque. Perhaps because of this inner erosion, Teddy had little desire to call attention to himself. He was obsessed with the idea that people might notice the slight telltale disfigurements set deeply into his face, the aftermaths of a prolonged adolescent acne. No amount of cosmetic facial powders were able to conceal these blemishes. And, as much as he expressed horror at his appearance, he rejected a dermatologist's advice to take collagen injections to remedy the unevenness. His own "ugliness" became the major ingredient of what made other men sexually appealing to him.

Though considering himself unsightly, Teddy took pride in dressing like a latter-day preppy. He usually wore a slightly frayed tweed jacket, underlining an unkempt stylistic imperative.

E. Mark Stern, EdD, Columbia University, 1955, Diplomate in Clinical Psychology of the American Board of Professional Psychology, Fellow of the American Psychological Association, is Professor, Graduate Division of Pastoral and Family Counseling, Iona College, New Rochelle, NY. He is in private practice in New York City and Clinton Corners, NY. Mailing address: 215 East 11 St., New York, NY 10003.

There was another therapist a year before we met to whom he first admitted to what he termed "off the board" homosexual fantasies. When I made my own inquiry into these fantasies, he stood up, stared down at me and asked: "How can I trust that you'd ever understand the pain that I've been enduring?" I said that he could choose or not choose to take a risk.

"Yes," he grudgingly allowed, he would be willing to make another appointment, but exactly 24 hours before the scheduled meeting, he canceled. The message said that he'd call again. I wasn't too sure he would, but exactly one week later, he phoned. There was apprehension in his voice. "Can I have that Wednesday time for the following week?" I could not accommodate him, but we finally settled for a very early morning appointment on the following day.

He began by saying that he might have trouble telling me about the specifics of his fantasy life. This latest return to therapy was in response to anxiety grown beyond his control. He wanted to gain some degree of control and self-confidence. Slowly, as if sorting out playing cards in a game of solitaire, he selectively began to recite his major concerns.

He said he was ashamed of being unusually attracted by "leperously" looking men. "A bad joke played on me by God." He looked square into my face: "Are you shocked?" he asked.

"All of us," I said, "live a good part of our lives in our fantasies. You've shared feelings and sensations which are sacred to you. If you sense my being shocked, perhaps it's because your fantasies are so powerful."

"Thank you," he said, "I think you not only sense my burden, but you also respect me." Our interaction freed him sufficiently to speak about what he called one of his more "bizarre seizures." It had taken place some months before. He had taken a stroll in a somewhat deserted waterside section of a familiar city park. It was dusk. He knew he was looking for a sexual contact. Nothing had developed. There was a moment of mixed relief when he felt able to leave the park. But no sooner had he changed direction than he was signaled over by an overly obese man whom he described as "Having been in his late 50s or early 60s." The man was hypnotic and Teddy felt literally locked into his stare. The man said nothing as he unzipped his fly and exposed his semi-erect penis. At first, Teddy felt a fascination followed by rush of massive anxiety. He fled the scene. Imagery of this near rendezvous flooded his consciousness. He masturbated throughout the night. The next morning, he contemplated suicide.

It was no easier the following afternoon. He returned to the park, "wasting" many hours that day and many days thereafter, searching aimlessly for "a rematch of that botched up encounter." We sat in silence as I weighed my options. I decided that for the time being, just my presence was all that was needed. Any other action would have betrayed his trust.

We met twice a week for well over a month during the early phases of therapy. During this inauguration period, he relayed his sense of growing helplessness: "I feel duped by the sordidness of my life." He did, however, say that since seeing me, he felt less urgency to "cruise" for sexual purposes.

Eight weeks into our work, Teddy called to postpone any additional appointments for at least a month. He said that his job might be taking him out of the city. I heard nothing from him for some weeks. Then quite late one night my phone rang. I would not have picked up the receiver had there not been a possibility of an emergency in my family. There was silence after my guarded hello. I held on. Soon: a gasping cry on the other end. Sensing the intonations, I asked: "Is that you, Teddy?" There was a quick hang-up. He called the next day for an appointment. When I saw him, I asked again: "Was that you on the phone?" He averted my glance, but did not answer.

"Would you mind if I use the couch from now on?" he asked. I said that he could proceed in any way that he felt most comfortable.

Yes, he admitted, it was him. He was astonished that Z would have known that. "I wouldn't have been able to tolerate it from anyone else," he said. But by now he had concealed his face against the side of the couch.

"So why with me?" I asked.
"I felt that you would never betray me."

I was uncomfortable with such trust, but knew from his prior abrupt interruption of the process that it was all conditional.

I proceeded with caution. As might have been expected, Teddy missed his next two sessions. There were superficial excuses followed by his asking: "Do you see any reason for my continuing with these meetings?"

I stumbled: "I don't quite know how to answer. I'll be here for you or not be here for you as you decide." Later: "You must have had good reason for asking me about you continuing in therapy?"

"Well," he hesitated, "I have to tell you that I don't really ever feel very safe here." Once said, he began to fill me in on his early life.

Teddy was the youngest of two boys. There had been an earlier son who died at 10 years of age who had been named Anthony–"Teddy" for short. The next son, Jerold, never had a nickname. The last, born the year after Anthony died was Teddy. He made it clear that his name was not intended to be short for Anthony.

His father was a building contractor with limited formal education, but "awfully well read." He was born the only son of a working-class couple in an industrial community. He was never very affectionate, but always respected in the community as "a reliable family man." From looking at a snapshot of him dating back to when Teddy was a child, he had a telltale jeer written all over his face. Teddy was intimidated by his father's self-righteous dismissal of anything or anyone "who got in his way." There were no shared events. "My father was all business and impatience." He did, however, recall his fascination with once looking at his father's penis while he was urinating. "He had that knowing smirk on his face as he quickly tucked it away in his fly. . . . He knew, he knew, and had nothing but disdain for me."

Mother came from a large Eastern European family. She attended parochial schools and later studied music. Throughout his childhood, she served as principal organist in a large urban church. Teddy recalls being morbidly curious about her numerous private piano students. "I think I was infatuated with each of the adult male pupils. I guess I fantasized her stealing kisses from them. I would sometimes imagine being invited in to watch while they made out with each other. I would feign jealousy while picturing Mama licking their big fingers." As he spoke, he closed his eyes, ashamed and worried about my reaction. Yet on some level, he seemed to want to catch me in the thrill he had experienced. She was frequently depressed, and during these times intimidating to both boys. As a result, Teddy claimed that he felt too clumsy to learn how to play the piano from her.

"Were they grieving for Anthony? You know a child's imagination can replay past impressions in a way which is both haunting and exciting."

"Quite possible. I live in a fog of forbiddens." Whatever the fog, it was enough to encourage Teddy to camouflage his identity. "I always felt like some sort of slim resemblance to a boy I never knew. There were pictures of Anthony in albums, but none on the mantle. It certainly was a house of mourning, though I never sensed my parents felt that there was very much special about Anthony." There were times that Teddy consoled himself with pretending that he was Anthony's opposite. Jerold, on the other hand, was alternatively seen as the "blockhead" and "darling" of the family. Jerold's relationship to Teddy was distant, angry and calculating.

Jerold's friend Kenneth was a constant presence in their house. He, along with Jerold, bore down heavily on the younger Teddy. "I lived in total terror of Kenneth. He'd take vulgar liberties with me." The incidents were examples of coercive outrage which Kenneth became a party to. "There were times when he'd spit under the back collar of my shirt. And I can never forget the time he was eating at our house and whispered to me just after I had finished a tuna fish sandwich how he and Jerold had spit and wriggled their cocks all over it before it was served to me. It was all so underground. I can still see Jerold with his hand over his mouth muffling his stitches."

"Did you ever retaliate?"

"I might have wanted to vomit, but I held it in and began to take some sort of perverse pleasure from it all. Mind you, there was never a time I could not afford to be tight-lipped about Kenny. I feared that my complaints would further indict me with my parents. They thought that I was an odd duck anyway. And, to be honest, I felt in some strange way that I deserved it. I was your stereotypical coward. But I had the last word. After a while, I began to relish Kenny; sort of secretly worshiped him. I knew he sensed how I felt. He took more and more liberties with me. He'd grab onto the outline of his penis and just stare at me. He knew that I could barely turn away. And I would cook over it for days; imagine having Kenny stand over me and threaten to piss into my mouth."

"Was it always pleasurable?"

"In a way it was, but the thoughts would leave me feeling really disturbed and hating myself. But I just couldn't stop."

"Did your parents ever get wind of what was going on?"

"I was plenty fearful that if they did find out that they might have repudiated me. My parents (they were still alive at the time of his therapy) have always been sharp. I've felt unworthy as long as I can remember. I felt like a sham—a counterfeit. But I tried never to let on. The admission that I was being mocked by any other kid was something I never let on about. It was easy to do since neither one of them wanted to be imposed on."

Shame had completely encircled Teddy's boyhood. Kenneth was not the end of his being prey. There had been groups of angry boys. Teddy recalled barely retreating from threats of castration by his peers. Although he dreaded these boys, he did attend the day camp's annual "sleepaway." While there, a somewhat older teen-ager, acting as the assistant counselor, came across Teddy wandering in an out-of-bounds wooded area. "I was just trying to get away from the others. He was urinating when he saw me. Let's face it, we were involved in a sort of secret follow-the-leader game. It was never stated, but we both knew we knew. He was a peculiar kid himself. He asked me what I was up to and offered to rub insect repellent over my body if I got naked. I was afraid at the time, but still kick myself for refusing. Somehow I associate the whole incident with slim odd shapes. He had an odd shape and I was as skinny as a rod."

"Did this bother you?" I asked. On the contrary, Teddy admitted to being irresistibly attracted by the boy's odd looks.

"I remember walking back to the campsite with him in absolute silence. When we returned none of the others paid attention to me. By that time they were engrossed in ghost stories. I couldn't get that whole experience out of my mind. I relived it for years." But as he got into the memory, it became clearer that through these reveries, he sought to create opportunities for the older boy to stand-in as his rescuer.

"For years," said Teddy, "I regretted not allowing him to rub my body. He would haunt my daydreams and take it to the extreme of enjoying visions of his urinating and defecating on me. It made me feel protected."

"I can understand that," I said. "After he deposited his waste products on you, you'd have smelled enough to repel all of your detractors?"

"But I'd still get sick at the thought of myself," even though he chose not to want to let go of "these maggots" enshrined in his fantasies.

We discussed the probability of his own self-betrayal. After all, his fantasies, though undermining, served him well by their power to transform the disparagements of others into rare pleasures. His construction of a personal victimizing reality, far more haunting than the attacks of others, had become locked into a danger-filled defensive posture.

This posture had ultimately become the foundation for most of Teddy's gratifications. What would "almost happen" in his fantasies guided him into hours of obsession. Teddy became mesmerized by ugliness and overpowered by a strangely satisfying protective presence. These masochistic images allowed him the latitude of bearing with the flawed uncertainties of his existence.

Teddy's fantasies were eventually acted out. An incident reminiscent of his day-camp overnight happened during the course of a company outing in a large city park. Never feeling comfortable in the presence of others, Teddy thought to explore the periphery of the picnic area which he sensed to be a possible meeting ground for homosexual encounters. As circumstances developed, he approached an inebriated derelict, clearly years older than Teddy.

Teddy, stimulated by the man's unwashed stench, paid him a few dollars to "pose" with his pants down. Teddy performed oral sex on the man, and during the act worried that the man might be a "mass murderer." Fearful excitement ruled the brief encounter. "Even now, years later," he said, "I'm unable to rid my brain of that guy. . . . Given the most far-out scenario, I'd do anything for him; expose myself to physical danger like walking barefoot on coals; I'd support him for the rest of his life if I could afford it."

The memory and support of this experience allowed Teddy some relief from his boredom and restlessness. But at what price?

"If he happened to be a mass murderer, doesn't that make it probable that he'd take pleasure in your being 'dead'?"

"I thought of that," he said. "He appeared from the dead, but his bodily smells and moisture became my life and pleasure."

"Have you gone back to try to find him?"

"In away, kind of half-heartedly. I've been too terrified to really look. In my craziest moments, I think he could be part some sort of setup. You know, the kind of situation in which you get trapped?"

"So why go?" I posed my question to be obviously naive. "Is he like a drug?"

"Even more powerful in this case. The guy seemed to know exactly what I wanted."

"Unlike either of your parents, but somehow like Kenneth? People who have been deprived of basic early respect can easily learn to be gratified, even as they fall prey to their betrayers."

He nodded his consent, and was understandably shaken by my comment. He hid his head with a pillow as he spoke of his fear of being stranded and homeless: "Sometimes I think I'd kill myself before letting that happen."

"And then be like your brother who died?" I had been wondering whether Anthony's death might have involved some foul play. As I was soon to learn, the boy had actually disappeared for several days before his body was found in a nearby bird sanctuary.

"Was the murderer ever found?" I asked. From all indications, his brother died at the hands of a self-confessed child molester. The accused, who had since died himself, might not have been the actual killer. There had been serious doubts at the trial. But even dubious justice had to be done.

Relating what he knew of the incident provoked Teddy to further lament about his own life. He said he knew that he was a constant appendage of his dead brother. This had been a dual union. Would he too die in the trap of victimized seduction?

Compelling themes of death flowed evenly with life promising forces. Teddy needed to know that his fantasies served him in his personal struggle for believable symbolizations of meaning and continuity (Lifton, 1979). In this regard, what he ultimately came to expect of his therapy was the transformation of troublesome visions into enhanced potentialities. Because of this I was inclined to help him craft essential links with the past in order to facilitate new paradigms.

Teddy's self-degrading fantasies, although entwined with the stuff which makes for crippling anxiety, were his only intimations of his existence as a viable personality. By becoming the shadow of Anthony, Teddy established some degree of psychic cohesiveness. From a therapeutic vantage, Teddy needed to know that his attractions, although filled with misery and self-destructive fantasies, were, nevertheless, invoked by him on behalf of the restoration of his life. As undermining as his acting out behaviors appeared to be, they helped extend his emotional resources. In order to affirm an identity, his raptures invoked an unfortunate union with his dead brother.

A person's history can be seen in more than one light. The more extensive the view, the greater the potentiality for healing. To better facilitate his claim on an identity distinct from his brother, Teddy needed to see the past in a new light in order to seek a broader based continuity with it.

As our relationship deepened, I decided to mention the erstwhile dermatologist who had advised him on the repair of his post-acne scars: "Like him," I said, "I too have a sense that the earlier wounds and debilitations can be newly addressed." My words were slow and deliberate. A new level had been reached. Teddy became engaged. "Suppose, just suppose," I said, "that your Mom wanted only the very best of Anthony in you? Could that mean that she desired simply that you remain something of a son who she really wanted to see grow to adulthood?"

"Then she should not have plagued me with his nickname." I willingly agreed with him. And I hoped he had not felt that a name necessarily brought eternal condemnation with it. The important thing was that we had both come to agree that our work was reaching for newer beginnings.

Eventually we had come to the point of his taking responsibility for his own life despite the emotional ignorance of his parents. I suggested that he consider what it might mean to forgive them for the way they asked him to deal with their grief.

"That's asking a lot of me." Much later: "Of course I know that

that's what I have to do," he said, "but I wonder if they understand what their actions did to me?"

"What would that mean to you if they did," I asked.

"It might help us communicate, though I never could expose my off-the-wall attractions to them. . . . I think I might have to let them know that I've been strange because I had to be me, not Anthony."

"But being you begins with you. Much of your attraction lives out Anthony's destruction."

He began to speak about his father: "From what I understand, Dad had little interest in naming me. Anthony was after his father, my grandfather. I guess it was conveyed to me that I am just a nobody."

"That fact alone gives you the freedom to be who you want to be. Your Mom had an agenda, your Dad had lost all vestiges of hope. What about your brother?"

Jerold, who was six by the time Teddy was born, had a reputation for being weak-willed and slow. He had apparently never liked Anthony who was 4 years older. Teddy was likewise seen as an intruder.

Jerold's friends were all two to four years his junior. He was not well regarded by the parents of these friends. There had been several complaints about his bad influence on the neighborhood children. Neither of his own parents paid much attention to his passive aggressive manipulations. For all of it, Jerold was treasured by both parents. As far as Teddy was concerned, he might as well have been born into a fictional family for all the unreality of his parents.

The mention of either sibling was not easy for Teddy. Both brothers made it all the more imperative that he rescue his own identity. To have to replace a dead sibling brought the reality of personal dissolution that much closer. He went about as a person dead from the start. Teddy began to see his challenge as having to transcend being the remains of a brother mutilated by a violent death. He began to understand how his acne-scarred face provided him with even more license for living with thoughts of his own decomposure.

Teddy's perpetual declivity summoned up gory images. He had ultimately been betrayed by cooperating with self-destructive messages. For so long, he felt that he could in no way restrain the forces of death. He recalled being asked to scrub his father's back. It had

started out as an ordinary day on the beach, but for the debris that
had floated close to shore. Jelly fish and seaweed had washed close
to shore. His father's body was festooned with grime and stench. As
he scaled his father's hairy back with a washcloth, Teddy fastened
on to the idea of being a counterpart of the slime. He was then a
preadolescent, but the feeling evidenced a comforting familiarity
with sludge and phlegm. He recalled being ecstatic with his phan-
toms. It would have been too easy for him to blame his father for
not protecting him.

Teddy's masochistic obsessions prevented his disunion from the
family's betrayal by a still-unknown killer. The web was extensive,
disallowing each family member the capacity for feeling unmolest-
ed. The family had existed in bad faith. Treachery had been done
them, and each one became suspect of the other. There had been the
unspoken, undisplayed skeletons in the closet which haunted their
morale. Only betrayal had succeeded in amassing an elemental
relatedness. Because of this, Teddy chose not to disclose to anyone
in the family his being in therapy.

For a time, he saw our work as surreptitious, perhaps because I
refused to pathologize his fantasies. He said he felt safe because his
forbidden images were being respected.

I suggested that it was unfortunate for him to be so humiliated
because he happened to find beauty in the grotesque. "If you are
able to romance the grotesque, then perhaps that very capacity
could prime you for an even greater range of appreciation." Since
my reactions were caring and attentive, our therapy never promoted
an impasse. When he felt most unprotected and exposed, he knew
that I would not abandon him.

At long last, Teddy began to be feel motivated to shift from the
hold of his fantasies. There were noticeable shifts as he revised
contacts with his emotional roots along with growing signs of his
self-concern and personal awareness. "All the parts are there," I
assured him, "It's just learning to know that they can sort out in
newer creative ways." Grotesqueness became not an imprisonment,
but an opportunity for him to enjoy a repertoire of personal aesthet-
ics far greater than that which society dictates. His sensibility for
the extraordinary lived in a constructive relationship with the more
acceptably ordinary. He was on his way to knowing what it meant to

become more courageous and more tempered. He no longer needed masochism to affirm a false identity.

As I might have suspected, therapy ended several months after he changed his first name. We decided to create a ceremony in which I would be empowered to witness his renaming. He chose to be called Bruce. There were no other Bruces in his life. The name associated with "brute," but only for the time being. Bruce was agreeable in sound. It did not freely lend itself to an adult nickname. Documents had to be changed. His family seemed unconcerned, but helpful. I drew him a "before" and "after" cartoon which he said he'd treasure as his primary documentation of change.

In our final session, I asked him if he was scared. "Scared and excited," he replied. Therapy had helped him deal better with both sensations. Eventually Bruce married and had a daughter. Yet all did not necessarily go well. There were lapses, and with them he'd make appointments to "touch base" with me. His daughter had reached high school and word came that Bruce had been infected with the HIV virus. I tried to reach him, but he had moved.

I can only hope to think of Bruce as a man who proved that he could sometime move beyond the betrayals brought upon him, in large measure, by a great tragedy.

REFERENCE

Lifton, R.J. (1979). *The broken connection: On death and the continuity of life.* New York: Simon & Schuster.